A JOHN CATT PUBLICATION

Nimish Lad

SHIMAMURA'S

MARGE MODEL OF LEARNING

IN ACTION

IN ACTION SERIES

EDITOR **TOM SHERRINGTON**

WITH FOREWORD BY DANIEL WILLINGHAM
ILLUSTRATIONS BY OLIVER CAVIGLIOLI

A **WALKTHRUs** PRODUCTION

First Published 2021

by John Catt Educational Ltd,
15 Riduna Park, Station Road,
Melton, Woodbridge IP12 1QT

Tel: +44 (0) 1394 389850
Email: enquiries@johncatt.com
Website: www.johncatt.com

Illustrations by Oliver Caviglioli

ISBN: 978 1 913622 67 1

Set and designed by John Catt Educational Limited

SERIES FOREWORD
TOM SHERRINGTON

The idea for the *In Action* series was developed by John Catt's *Teaching WalkThrus* team after we saw how popular our *Rosenshine's Principles in Action* booklets proved to be. We realised that the same approach might support teachers to access the ideas of a range of researchers, cognitive scientists and educators. A constant challenge that we wrestle with in the world of teaching and education research is the significant distance between the formulation of a set of concepts and conclusions that might be useful to teachers and the moment when a teacher uses those ideas to teach their students in a more effective manner, thereby succeeding in securing deeper or richer learning. Sometimes so much meaning is lost along that journey, through all the communication barriers that line the road, that the implementation of the idea bears no relation to the concept its originator had in mind. Sometimes it's more powerful to hear from a teacher about how they implemented an idea than it is to read about the idea from a researcher or cognitive scientist directly – because they reduce that distance; they push some of those barriers aside.

In our *In Action* series, the authors and their collaborative partners are all teachers or school leaders close to the action in classrooms in real schools. Their strategies for translating their subjects' work into practice bring fresh energy to a powerful set of original ideas in a way that we're confident will support teachers with their professional learning and, ultimately, their classroom practice. In doing so, they are also paying their respects to the original researchers and their work. In education, as in so many walks of life, we are standing on the shoulders of giants. We believe that our selection of featured researchers and papers represents some of the most important work done in the field of education in recent times.

This *In Action* book is a perfect example of the value of asking a practising teacher to explore the classroom applications of a researcher's ideas. I was one of the many people, alongside Nimish Lad, delighted to discover Arthur Shimamura's eBook, where he sets out his MARGE model, via social media. The 'whole brain' model is fascinating, with each of the five elements of MARGE contributing to a deeper understanding of the learning process with implications for classroom practice. Nimish is one of the great enthusiasts in the world of 'edutwitter' sharing ideas and championing the work of others. I knew he'd be excited about this project and he has succeeded in delivering a superb account of MARGE In Action.

We were thrilled to have Arthur's endorsement for this book in its early stages and were all deeply saddened to hear that he passed away in October 2020. Daniel Willingham was instrumental in sharing Shimamura's work with the online teacher community so it is wonderful that he has contributed the lovely foreword, paying tribute to Arthur's contribution to the field.

FOREWORD BY DANIEL T. WILLINGHAM

In 1993, just out of graduate school, I attended a small meeting of memory researchers at the Cold Spring Harbor research campus. It was damn scary, as the attendees were all people whose work I had studied and revered. James Watson, the legendary molecular biologist and head of the facility at the time, sat in on some of the talks. I, one of two junior people there (why, why?) felt shaky and far out of my depth, an ensign who had blundered into a war-planning meeting of admirals.

At lunch the first day we were eating at a barracks-like mess hall (long tables, benches) and no one was speaking to me, which was fine, because I was sulking, thinking my talk that morning had gone over terribly. Art Shimamura sat down at my right with his tray. We hadn't met, but I of course knew who he was. We exchanged greetings, and ate in silence for a few minutes. Then Art turned to me and said, 'Do you know what I *especially* like about your work?'

You can understand why I remember that remark after 30 years, but as I was to later learn, this sort of comment was typical of Art. It wasn't just that he sought to make a junior researcher and stranger feel welcome and valued. He opened with a question, characteristic of his unquenchable curiosity.

Art Shimamura made profound contributions to the study of memory in the 1980s and 90s, especially on the question of the unity of memory. Is memory one thing, or should memory theory acknowledge multiple types of memory? If so, how would they be differentiated in theories? And what sort of evidence would be definitive? Art was one of a handful of researchers posing these questions in the early 1980s, and one of an even smaller set offering answers based on neuroscientific methods.

Like most great thinkers, Art had intellectual wanderlust, and he was not reluctant to indulge it. He went on to publish important work in visual perception, aesthetics, aging, and emotion. But towards the end of his career, he returned to memory with the publication of an ebook, *MARGE: A Whole-Brain Approach to Learning*. The title encapsulates what's so wonderful about the approach to teaching it describes: the book analyzes fundamental cognitive processes (memory, attention, motivation) but it's obvious that these processes are not independent of one another. If you change one, you may very well change others. It requires someone like Art with comprehensive knowledge of cognition as a whole, to anticipate those interactions, and to write about the processes of teaching and learning with them in mind.

But although Art was an award-winning college professor, he was not a K-12 teacher. How fortunate, then, that we have Nimish Lad to interpret the lessons of MARGE for this new audience. Lad has done a marvelous job of bringing the principles of MARGE to life in classroom contexts, with vivid case studies, such as bringing emotion into a biology lesson via the discussion of ethical issues like the use of stem cells. But for all the rich detail, Lad manages to stay focused on practical utility. I especially love the table that summarizes each chapter, reminding you of what's been described, what to do with it, and how it might go wrong.

A danger with a book like this is that the author might convince himself that he's carrying the banner of Truth into battle with the benighted, backed by the artillery of Science. There's none of that overconfident zeal to be found here. Lad does a beautiful job of explaining the principles of MARGE and then showing how they are compatible with multiple classroom practices and approaches.

I hope and expect you will enjoy this volume as much as I did. I think every teacher will find something in it that will expand their mind and challenge them to reflect on their practice.

Daniel T. Willingham

Keswick, VA

April 23, 2021

TABLE OF CONTENTS

students so well. I would like to thank these colleagues, and the hard-working teachers who openly invite me into their classrooms, be that first thing on a Monday morning, or last thing on a Friday afternoon. The work you do will always reshape my thinking. Redwell Primary School and Park Junior School in Wellingborough, especially Natasha Kelf and David Tebbutt, have been fantastic in ensuring I have had a wide view of education across all phases.

Steve, Becky, Jon, David, Hannah, Matt and Alice; the long conversations we have had on Tuesday nights have framed my thinking, and set me off in a direction to think more about much of what has been written within this book. Chris, you helped me write a timetable so I could write this!

Finally, but most importantly, I am indebted to my wonderfully patient, smart and thoughtful wife Pooja, and my joyous daughter Freya, both of whom have put up with me disappearing for hours. Without the support of all my family, who have heard me talk about nothing else but the process of learning for the last 18 months, this book would never have been written.

INTRODUCTION

The process of learning, and specifically the science behind it, has become an area of great interest in recent years. I had a basic understanding of cognitive science from my studies at university, but I had spent little time trying to apply this to my teaching practice. Towards the end of 2018 this changed, when by chance I was lucky enough to stumble across a free ebook that redefined my view of the learning process. *MARGE: A Whole-Brain Learning Approach for Students and Teachers*[1] by Professor Arthur Shimamura (Professor Emeritus of Psychology from the University of California, Berkeley) instantly grabbed my attention as a model for maximising learning.

Shimamura's book is particularly fascinating, as it links what is known about the neuroscience of the brain and the cognitive science of how we learn. Rooted in research around how the brain works when processing new information and recalling prior knowledge, MARGE is a powerful set of principles that can be used effectively within the classroom. Each of the five letters in the acronym – Motivate, Attend, Relate, Generate and Evaluate – was looked at in detail, and linked to cognitive science. While the original book was written for use in universities, this *In Action* book aims to bring MARGE into the classroom, applying the principles to all ages and stages, from Early Years Foundation Stage (EYFS) through to Key Stage 5. Examples from practicing teachers are used to exemplify how each principle can be seamlessly integrated into lessons, providing a clear model for how MARGE can affect the learning of students. The first section of this book will give an overview of the key parts of the brain involved with the learning process and how MARGE links with them, while the rest of the book will discuss practical strategies for each principle in detail.

Learning and top-down processing

To understand the role the brain plays in the learning process, we must first define what we mean by learning. Daniel Willingham has mentioned that most definitions of learning are interpreted within the context of the writer's theory, for example Kirschner, Sweller and Clark's definition, 'Learning is a change

1. Shimamura, A. (2018). *MARGE: A whole-brain learning approach for students and teachers.* Retrieved from https://bit.ly/3rPxulE

in long-term memory' is set within the context of Cognitive Load Theory.[2] Shimamura defines learning as 'Our ability to acquire knowledge from sensory experiences'[3] and goes on to describe three types of learning:

- **Perceptual learning,** where learning happens through exposure to a variety of sensory experiences, such as learning to distinguish between differing tones of music.
- **Conceptual learning** (or academic learning), where newly acquired facts are linked to prior knowledge, which is much of what happens in the classroom.
- **Skill learning,** where practice, trial and error leads to progression, such as learning to play a new piece of music.

MARGE, while applicable to all areas of learning, is specifically applicable to conceptual learning. In psychological terms the process of acquiring knowledge can be described as bottom-up or top-down processing.

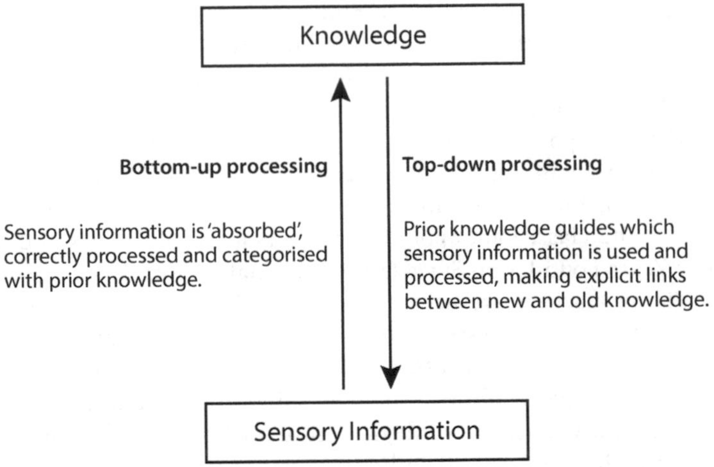
Knowledge
Bottom-up processing
Sensory information is 'absorbed', correctly processed and categorised with prior knowledge.
Top-down processing
Prior knowledge guides which sensory information is used and processed, making explicit links between new and old knowledge.
Sensory Information

Top-down processing is the most efficient form of learning. This mode of processing avoids sensory overload, as a wide base of prior knowledge is used to guide which sensory information is attended to and processed.

Bottom-up processing is inefficient and can lead to sensory overload. In this

2. Willingham, D. T. (2017, June 26). *On the definition of learning.* Retrieved from https://bit.ly/2PZGV4z
3. Shimamura, A. (2018), p1

mode, sensory information is 'absorbed', as if by diffusion, into memory. This leads to minimal meaningful links being made, and any knowledge gained being a set of disparate unconnected elements.

Top-down processing allows a key feature of the learning process to come into play; the idea of knowing what needs to be paid attention to, and therefore what information can be filtered out. Imagine sitting in a university lecture, listening to the lecturer talking through an idea. Every now and again, an anecdote is thrown in to keep the lecture interesting. If all processing was bottom-up, this would lead to you trying to memorise the anecdote, absorbing that information as a set of facts with no clear links to any knowledge you previously had. However, by activating prior knowledge as part of top-down processing, new and relevant information being discussed in the lecture can be linked together quickly, while the anecdotes (if they are not relevant) can be filtered out.

A key point here is the important role that prior knowledge plays in the process. In EYFS, including reception, pupils often learn through play. While this seems like bottom-up processing, careful observations of the exceptional work of early years teachers shows that through clear instruction, questioning and prompting, learning becomes a top-down process.

Active learning is a phrase that has been bounced around the educational sector, but it is not about getting out of your seats and moving around the room or completing a task. The idea of active learning could be rephrased as 'cognitively active learning'. This would lead to a different set of questions being asked when we observe learning: Are students actively engaging with the learning process? Are they top-down processing? Are they bottom-up processing?

A good example of this is discussing with students what they do when given a textbook and assigned pages to read. Students who are top-down processing will attempt to get a gist of the content first so that they can bring relevant prior knowledge to the front of their mind, allowing them to attend to relevant content in the text. Students who are bottom-up processing will read the textbook with no clearly defined strategy to link what they are taking in to any prior knowledge.

The insightful part of Shimamura's book is the link it makes between neuroscience and cognitive science. It is important to note here that while an understanding of the neuroscience behind the brain is interesting, it is not required knowledge for applying the principles of MARGE. With that in mind, the following section will cover a brief overview of the neuroscience Shimamura discusses, before we move on to how it can affect our teaching.

THE BRAIN

While this chapter is interesting and provides a framework around which Shimamura has built his MARGE model of learning, it is only included for background knowledge purposes. Further detail can be found in Shimamura's original book.

Much has been said and written about **cognitive science** and its application in the classroom, but too often it has been confused with **neuroscience**. While cognitive science deals with more abstract processes such as cognition, neuroscience deals with more tangible effects such as changes in the electrical signals within the brain. These two fields have found an area of overlap since the advent of fMRI, functional magnetic resonance imaging, which can be used to map regions of the brain that become active throughout the learning process.

When discussing the brain, it is important to understand that the parts of the brain do not operate in isolation in the learning process. MARGE is a whole-brain approach to learning, quite different from some other ideas, such as learning styles, or left-brain right-brain dominance theory. The various parts of the brain do not lend themselves to any single preferred method of learning for an individual, as stated by Shimamura:

> *Over-indulgent practitioners often fall prey to a modern-day form of phrenology – if we can only boost activity in these brain regions, we can solve the problem of poor student learning. Even worse are those practitioners who use brain regions as markers for 'styles' of learning – are you a left-brain (verbal), right-brain (spatial), back-brain (perceiving), or front-brain (thinking) learner? ... Efficient learning and retention depends on coordinated brain activity in a multitude of brain regions.*[4]

Structures and functions of parts of the brain

A summary of the key features of functions of the brain include:

- **Prefrontal cortex (PFC)** – controls the executive functions such as attention, decision making and the maintenance of working memory.

4. Shimamura, A. (2018, July 21). *The power and pitfalls of brain-based learning programs.* Retrieved from https://bit.ly/3mmOE9g

- **Occipital cortex** – where visual imagery is processed.
- **Heschl's gyrus** – where auditory information is processed.
- **Medial temporal lobe (MTL)** – binds information into episodic[5] memory.
- **Cerebral cortex** – where conceptual knowledge[6] is stored.
- **Midbrain** – contains the rewards circuit; linked to motivation and memory.

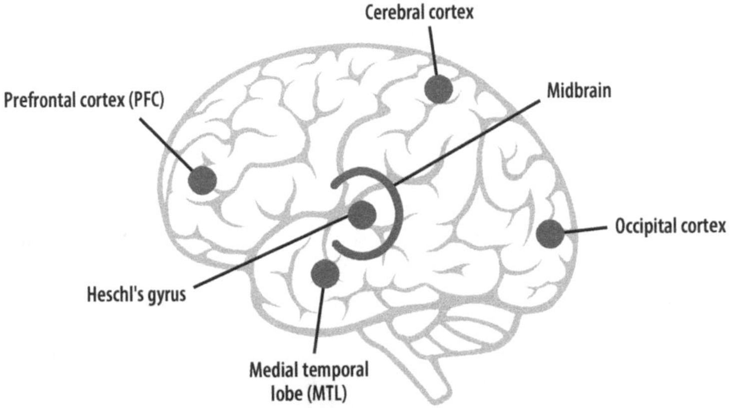
Cerebral cortex
Prefrontal cortex (PFC)
Midbrain
Occipital cortex
Heschl's gyrus
Medial temporal lobe (MTL)

When reading Shimamura's MARGE, there are five key conclusions that can be drawn:

- To ensure students remain **motivated** to learn, we need to foster epistemic curiosity, activating the midbrain reward pathways.
- Consideration must be given to the amount and layout of text being presented, as well as what is being said, to ensure the PFC knows what to **attend** to.
- The delivery of new concepts needs to allow our MTL to **relate** new information to existing information.
- Build in opportunities for students to **generate** connections in the cerebral cortex, through repeated usage and reactivation of learned information.
- Without the PFC focussing on the right stimulus and **evaluating** the knowledge we have gained, the process of learning becomes obsolete.

5. Episodic memories; recollected memories related to events and experiences.
6. Conceptual knowledge (declarative knowledge); facts, processes, attributes and how they are related.

Shimamura discusses that the midbrain is the site of the production of dopamine, which has some control of motivational salience; the degree to which a person is motivated or repelled by an event, object or outcome. Imaging of the brain when patients have been subjected to pleasurable processes, such as listening to music, indicate that areas of the brain associated with efficient learning, such as the PFC, are linked to the reward circuit in the midbrain.

When attempting to motivate students as part of the learning process, Shimamura discusses the idea of curiosity as key for engaging the reward circuit. It is important to consider if the curiosity we are fostering is epistemic – wanting to go deep and learn more about a subject – rather than diverse – wanting to experience a range of new ideas.

To ensure students remain motivated to learn, we need to foster epistemic curiosity, activating the midbrain reward pathways.

The PFC makes up about 28% of the brain. It is involved in the processing of our thoughts; controlling what we are thinking about and therefore our attention, which in turn fosters in us the belief that we have control over what we pay attention to. While reading this book, if I asked you to listen carefully to see if you could hear a bird outside the window, you would instantly switch your attention to search for that sound. You would no longer be focussed on what you were reading on this page, your PFC would not be processing information from this book alone, and the learning process would be impeded.

Research has shown that in children, the **executive function** – the ability to choose and filter sensory inputs – is not as well developed as in adults. When children were presented with cards and asked to sort them by colour, the task was completed easily. When they were presented with the same cards but were asked to sort by shape, they found the process much more difficult, because they had to switch their attention from shape to colour. This demonstrates the importance of attention, and the ability to switch attention, in the learning process.[7]

When you are fully attending to the information you are receiving, your PFC allows you to categorise, sort and store incoming information and critically, make links with pre-existing information. In this way the PFC is making decisions about information being received based on what is already known.

Within the classroom, students are receiving information through two main channels: sight through the occipital cortex and sound through the Heschl's gyrus. Both are constantly sending information to the cerebral cortex and PFC

7. Doebel, S. (2019). *How your brain's executive function works and how to improve it.* [Video file] Retrieved from https://youtu.be/qAC-5hTK-4c

about the world around us. Interestingly, the occipital cortex sends information via two routes: a dorsal path for spatial processing, and a ventral path for processing the object. This has great implications for how we consider not only what we are saying while we deliver content, but also what we see written and how it is presented spatially.

Consideration must be given to the amount and layout of text being presented, as well as what is being said, to ensure the PFC knows what to attend to.

The MTL stores episodic memories. The storage of conceptual knowledge – the knowledge we are most often teaching students – requires a process called memory consolidation. This process involves relevant prior knowledge being activated before it is then related to information being received. This gives students meaning to what they are learning. As stated by Efrat Furst, 'Meaning is generated when the new concept is associated with other concepts that the learner is already familiar with, in a way that makes sense to the learner. The learner can now understand the meaning of the new concept.'[8]

The delivery of new concepts needs to allow our MTL to relate new information to existing information.

Imaging of the brain has shown that the PFC and the MTL are activated when we have to self-generate content. Repeating this process repeats memory consolidation, leading to stronger links in long-term memory. This also allows learners to make new links between areas of knowledge.

The analogy of the maze is useful to consider here; self-generation is analogous to the process of going through a maze time and time again, finding new ways through, new paths, and linking to other landmarks that may exist within it.

Build in opportunities for students to generate connections in the cerebral cortex, through repeated usage and reactivation of learned information.

Where the PFC has been damaged, patients have not lost the ability to store memories, rather they lose the ability to use memories. It is useful, as Shimamura discusses, to think of the PFC as the conductor of an orchestra, dictating the pace and tempo of thought, calling on different parts of the brain at varying times to recall specific memories. It plays an important role in metacognitive processes, as through the process of recall we can test the strength of our understanding of specific topics.

Without the PFC focussing on the right stimulus and evaluating the knowledge we have gained, the process of learning becomes obsolete.

8. Furst, E. (2021). *Learning in the brain*. Retrieved from https://bit.ly/3rSY3Go

MARGE

Efficient learning and retention depends on coordinated brain activity in a multitude of brain regions.[9]

Any model which attempts to describe the process of learning needs to consider it as a whole-brain process and understand that efficient learning and retention needs coordination between different parts of the brain, which is clearly shown by neuroscience. Five statements summarised at the end of the key paragraphs in the last section of this chapter relate to the letters in the acronym of MARGE, bridging the gap between neuroscience and cognitive science, allowing us to begin to discuss how this can affect classroom practice.

Motivate	The need for motivation to be in place to engage the reward circuit
Attend	To ensure the PFC is focussing on the right sensory input
Relate	Make links between new knowledge and prior knowledge
Generate	Reactivating prior knowledge and forging new links
Evaluate	Checking that the knowledge gained is correct, embedded in long-term memory and can be applied to novel situations

The model has a powerful application, especially as we consider the journey that a student goes through when they learn a concept.

Imagine a student who has always had an interest in Ancient Greece, this could have come about from a trip to Greece in their younger years, or a visit to the British Museum. When presented with the question 'How did the ancient Greeks change the world?' the student is **motivated** to know more about this subject area. They can draw on their own experiences and have a curiosity to deepen their learning. By being taught ideas in small chunks, such as the impact of the ancient Greeks on the alphabet, democracy, architecture or sport, the student would know exactly what part of their experience of the modern world they would need to **attend** to. By **relating** chunks of their knowledge of the Greeks, they could build a detailed mental image of what life was like at that time; new links could be **generated** as they compared their understanding

9. Shimamura, A. (2018, July 21). *The power and pitfalls of brain-based learning programs.* Retrieved from https://bit.ly/3mmOE9g

of ancient Greece to the modern world, comparing and contrasting the ways in which the two societies live their lives. As the student returns to the ancient Greeks, interleaved with different topics in the curriculum, they will be able to **evaluate** the strength of their knowledge, ensuring it is embedded rather than just having a familiarity with the concept.

While this is a brief overview of a student journey and understanding of the ancient Greeks, it demonstrates the power of a whole-brain learning approach as modelled by MARGE.

CHAPTER 1
M: MOTIVATE

The trick to motivation is to expand the spectrum of pleasure-seeking experiences and push ourselves into new learning situations.[10]

?

Shimamura says:
Motivate yourself and others to learn:[11]

- Explore new environs – take a walk around a town or a park.
- Field trip – visit a museum, historic landmark, or other cultural centre.
- Get thinking – know your schema and ask engaging questions.
- Get emotional – ask the 'aesthetic' question.
- Learn through storytelling – engage yourself with dramatic tales.
- Use web-based resources.

10. Shimamura, A. (2018), p10
11. Shimamura, A. (2018), p11

Within this chapter, these areas will be linked to the following strategies to encourage students to be motivated while learning:

- Big picture questions.
- Harness storytelling.
- Aesthetic questions.
- Exploring new places and new ideas.

Why do we need to motivate pupils?

Without students who are motivated, ensuring learning takes place in the classroom is incredibly difficult. Low motivation will lead to poor levels of engagement with the content being delivered and at best, passive learning. This is the first hurdle teachers must overcome as part of the learning process.

Two types of motivation often discussed are intrinsic and extrinsic motivation. Intrinsic motivation is when a student is driven by their own need to improve, while extrinsic motivation is where a student is motivated by external factors, such as rewards.

Clearly both types of motivation are built in to the structure of schools. However, in terms of the learning process, developing intrinsic motivation is key. Curriculum design needs to provide an opportunity for pupils to develop a love for learning about a subject through acquiring a carefully crafted, interconnected, deep bank of knowledge. This love for learning comes from having the knowledge to open doors to the wider topics within a subject.

When discussing why students are motivated cognitively to learn a specific topic, it is useful to consider what has led you to read this book.

What is it that made you pick up this book? Is it that you have an interest in understanding the process of learning and want to know more about it? Have you been to a lecture, or watched a talk on YouTube that got you interested in the science of learning? Have you understood part of the story behind learning, such as motivation and attention, and are keen to learn more? Why, at this stage of your career, is it so important to you that you take the time to read a book about how students learn?

These are the same types of question that may go through a student's mind when they are being taught. We are all aware that often students question what they are being taught: Why am I being taught this? Why is this topic important to me? Why do I need it when I am older?

The key to motivating pupils to learn a specific concept can be driven through tapping into their curiosity around the subject: epistemic curiosity. Ask effective questions and tell them the narrative of the subject by showing them how what they are learning is relevant to the bigger picture of their lives. Tell the story of the development of the concept, asking questions about how the content affects students' thoughts and feelings. Pique their curiosity by showing them a wider knowledge of the topic, broadening their interests and experiences.

As Shimamura says, this will expand the spectrum of pleasure-seeking activities, ensuring that students are not only curious to know and do more, but are motivated to dive deep into a subject and learn what really makes it tick.

The main focus of this chapter is to help you understand how we as teachers can motivate our students in the moment, in the lesson, to want to learn more about the topic at hand. Shimamura suggests the following strategies, which are supported by his understanding of the neuroscience of motivation:

1. **Big picture questions** – ask engaging questions that cover large areas of knowledge.
2. **Harness storytelling** – engage with the narratives within your subject.
3. **Aesthetic questions** – ask emotional questions about how students feel about concepts.
4. **Exploring new places and new ideas** – engaging in our culturally rich environment.

Why should we use big picture questions?

By asking big picture questions (also known as 'fertile questions') we are able to tease out information about what is already known while also providing a road map for the students' overarching schema; they now have an idea of how things will link together, leading to them feeling motivated to learn.

As teachers we must have an understanding of what exists in students' schema so we can add to it in a coherent manner, as doing anything else would harm any motivation they have. Consider walking into a lesson where you have no prior understanding of the topic being discussed. Instantly you would be on the back foot in terms of motivation and learning. Big picture questions work against this by activating students' prior knowledge, allowing them to feel success as they add new knowledge to it.

Big picture questions can be used incorrectly. Back in 2008, superheroes were again becoming popular with students. Being a fan myself, I had the idea of creating a unit of work around the big question of 'How do superheroes link to waves?'. Links were made between superpowers and waves of the electromagnetic spectrum as well as sound waves. A presentation was created to show at the start of each lesson to introduce the new superhero, the new waves they linked to and how this all joined together in the larger theme for the unit. Only when it was too late did I realise that while I succeeded in motivating the pupils, all I motivated them to do was find more links between physics and movies!

A key problem with how I went about this process was that I used a question to decide the content to be taught; I had decided I wanted to find a way to link superheroes to science. When deciding on these types of questions, content is king. Careful consideration needs to be taken regarding whether the content you are trying to deliver, in the sequence you intend to deliver it, can sit within a big question; does the big question drive your sequencing or is your sequencing deciding whether you need a big question?

How can we use big picture questions?

When redesigning my big question for this unit of work, I first considered the content being covered: electromagnetic and sound waves and their uses and dangers. This leant itself to the following big picture question: How are visible and invisible waves used by humans to improve the quality of life and how can they be dangerous? I could then map out the sequence of lessons under this overarching question.

How are visible and invisible waves used by humans to improve the quality of life and how can they be dangerous?

- Different types of waves: transverse and longitudinal, which are visible/invisible.
- Sound waves, including infrasound and ultrasound, how they travel and how they are used.
- Waves within the electromagnetic spectrum and their properties.
- The uses and dangers of each of the waves within the electromagnetic spectrum, specifically regarding how they are used in improving technology and the quality of life.

Each part of the content delivered can be linked back to the original question. Students can actively see themselves progressing through the content, gaining the intrinsic motivation which drives them through the learning process. As Neil Almond states in his chapter of Claire Sealy's *The ResearchED guide to the curriculum*, 'The curriculum needs to be planned carefully so that key ideas and concepts are continually revisited, remembered and built upon'.[12] Find those repeating themes that you can revisit with your students, and frame schema interrogating big picture questions around them.

Big picture questions in action

- In **geography** the big picture question 'Why do people live in a danger zone?' can be used to motivate future learning into migration, natural disasters, global economies, tourism and trade.
- In **KS1** the big picture question of 'Is a tree alive?' can be used to motivate learning about the life process.
- In **physical education** the big picture question of 'What affects an elite sportsperson's performance?' could motivate learning in areas such as nutrition and psychology.

Why should we harness storytelling?

Stories have a natural structure which can motivate students. Continually revisiting ideas is a feature of effective curriculum and lesson design, and also occurs in stories with narrative structures repeating themselves. Daniel Willingham, in his excellent book *Why Don't Students Like School?*, suggests lessons could have a design similar to that of stories:

> *The human mind seems exquisitely tuned to understand and remember stories; so much so that psychologists sometimes refer to stories as 'psychologically privileged,' meaning that they are treated differently in memory than other types of material. I'm going to suggest that organizing a lesson plan like a story is an effective way to help students comprehend and remember.*[13]

How can we harness storytelling?

Willingham goes on to describe the main features of a story. This acts as a useful lens when planning units of work, developing high quality explanations, or observing effective learning. He categorises the features of effective stories into four Cs of Causality, Conflict, Complications and Character:

12. Sealy, C. (2020). *The researchED guide to the curriculum*. Woodbridge: John Catt. p61
13. Willingham, D. T. (2010). *Why Don't Students Like School?* San Francisco: Jossey Bass. p51

Causality	Events do not concur randomly they are interconnected.
	Content should not appear randomly in a lesson, it should have been signposted early, or be connected to knowledge that preexists within the learners' schema.
Conflict	Events in a story involve progress towards an end goal, with difficulties along the way.
	The big picture is clear and students know what they are aiming towards. Areas of knowledge required as a prerequisite for learning are clear to students.
Complications	Sub-plots within the main story are there for a reason, enriching the experience.
	Anecdotes and asides within lessons are there to put the core knowledge delivered into a context to aid retention.
Character	Stories have characters that are clearly defined; the character traits appear naturally rather than being spelled out to the reader.
	Knowledge within a lesson has its own quality; this shows how it is linked to other knowledge. Think about the viewpoint from which you want your students to see the knowledge being delivered.

Causality is an often underexplored storytelling technique in lessons. By asking 'What's the story here?' we can aim to find the narrative within the content, show how it all stitches together and deliver it as a story.

An example could come from teaching the Archimedes principles. The core knowledge here is that upthrust is equal to the weight of fluid displaced. Through using ideas related to causality, we could explain this by saying 'When an object is immersed in a fluid, this **causes** some of the fluid to be displaced from its initial position. The displacement of this fluid occurs **because** a force is being applied on it, with this force being equal to the weight of fluid displaced. This **causes** a force to be applied back on the object. The size of the force on the object is equal to the weight of the fluid it displaced.'

The key to this is a carefully crafted explanation, told in the form of a story, that allows students to see how one event in a process is linked to the next. Without time being taken to ensure the explanation is clear, carefully sequenced and broken down into small steps, students will not be able to see the causal links that hold the process together.

The motivational aspect of learning through storytelling is clear to see. Just as good stories are interesting, easy to understand and allow inferences to be made about what will happen next, so is good learning. Students who experience this process will be motivated to learn more and do more with what they have learned.

Storytelling in action

- In **science** where the process of the electric bell can be told as a story, motivating students to better understand links of **causality** in physics.
- In **design technology** where students can learn about the **complications** faced in the creation of a product, such as Dyson vacuum cleaners, to motivate them to engage in the design process themselves.
- In **business** when learning about marketing and product development cycles, the story of **conflicting** and competing organisations can be told, for example Apple versus Samsung.
- In **geography** when we use **characters** to understand differing viewpoints about living in hazard locations, such as at the base of a volcano.

Case study: Art teaching in Year 3, Mai Bano

The following process can be used to harness storytelling as part of the process of teaching Van Gogh's work and the formal elements and techniques used in his paintings. First, students are told about the life of Vincent Van Gogh:

- Place deliberate thought into the perspective from which you want to deliver the knowledge to your students, for example share a picture book which captures the life of the artist and the experiences that inspired the creation of his most famous masterpieces.
- Use gestures and manipulate your tone of voice to reflect the emotions conveyed in the story.
- Heighten the sense of curiosity and excitement by making the storytelling interactive, for example pause to allow students to ask probing questions.
- Act out the character's responses as Van Gogh himself, enabling students to build an emotional connection and understand how his artwork was influenced by real-life events.

Following on from the story, students can apply the knowledge they have learned to scaled-down photographs of the artist's work. The connection between the knowledge about Van Gogh they have acquired through the story, and what they have learned about his techniques, will allow students to:

- Explain that the thick paint and brush strokes used in the paintings were known as impasto.

- Discuss that this was a result of how determined Van Gogh was as a post-impressionist artist to reflect movement and dimension in his art.
- Infer that through his use of colour Van Gogh conveyed the emotions he was experiencing at that particular time.
- Justify their reasoning by describing how the darker, sombre colours used in *Starry Night* mirrored how troubled Van Gogh felt towards the end of the story as he tried to come to terms with his mental health.

The character of Van Gogh, as he is introduced, gives students an idea of his qualities, and therefore allows them to link this to his art, and allows students to see Van Gogh's art from his own viewpoint. Through explaining about the complications he experienced, and how troubled he was, anecdotes are added, as is the idea of conflict.

*Mia Bano is a Class Teacher at Arden Primary School in Birmingham. Having an absolute passion for the creative arts, she is responsible for leading both art and design and design and technology across the school. She is a strong advocate for promoting diverse, multicultural children's literature in the classroom. She tweets at @MissBTeaches_*

Why should we use aesthetic questions?

Aesthetic questions engage students' emotions. This is a motivational technique which encourages pupils to participate in learning and organise their own thoughts, thus leading to deeper learning.[14]

In reception classes staff often ask a large number of aesthetic questions about texts that are being read or activities that are being completed. Students are continually having their thoughts challenged with questions such as:

- why do you like it or not like it?
- how do you think person x feels?
- why do you think this will happen next?
- who are your favourite characters? Why?

These questions are open-ended, do not have a right or wrong answer, engage the emotional circuits within the brain and force students to attend to and organise their knowledge.[15] They can be used to tease out the level of students'

14. Shimamura, A. (2020, June 5). *Do I Like It? Engage yourself with the 'aesthetic question.'* Retrieved from https://bit.ly/2PWLgpa
15. Shimamura, A. (2018), p11

understanding, allowing staff to celebrate success. A typical process that could happen in a reception classroom could be as follows:

Input with clear instruction from teacher based on key learning concept, for example number of shape.

↓

Play and learning activities are set up based around key learning concept, for example if number and number bonds, then skittles and bean bags are left out.

↓

As students play post-input, questions are asked about the learning to see whether students can apply knowledge from the input, for example if they knocked over two skittles and then four skittles, can they explain that these two numbers bond to six?

↓

Aesthetic questions are asked not only about the content, but about the learning process, for example 'How easily did you remember that number bond? Why do you think it is important to remember your number bonds when playing skittles?'

While many of these questions seem complicated, especially for a four- or five-year-old, practitioners in reception are exceptionally skilled at scaffolding, so that through play, students can demonstrate their learning. This style of learning is important in children's early development, and much of the reception curriculum is based on the development of communication and language, ensuring students feel confident in sharing their thoughts and ideas; aesthetic questions play a key role in developing this.

How can we use aesthetic questions?

Aesthetic questions are often asked in subjects such as art and photography, with the aim being to motivate students for future learning. Asking these types of questions encourages students to review the knowledge they have by engaging their thoughts and feelings over the work they have completed. The diagram below highlights a typical process of using aesthetic questions in art.

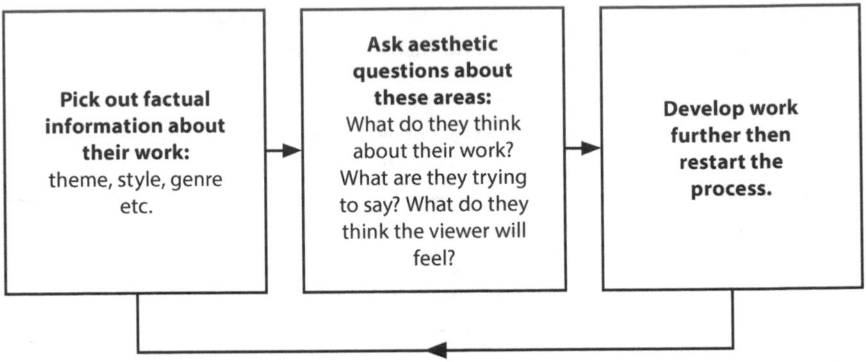
Pick out factual information about their work: theme, style, genre etc.
Ask aesthetic questions about these areas: What do they think about their work? What are they trying to say? What do they think the viewer will feel?
Develop work further then restart the process.

The role of aesthetic questions goes beyond an emotional feeling about a subject. Aesthetic questions can be used to motivate students to examine, challenge and support their own ideas, and therefore engage in the learning process.

Aesthetic questions in action

- In **English** to encourage students to think deeply about the feelings of characters in a novel, or techniques a writer is using, motivating them to form more thoughtful opinions.
- In **maths** when discussing techniques or approaches for a problem solving question, motivating students to further understand the processes and knowledge they are applying, for example why they prefer trial and error over other methods.
- In **science** when comparing different models or abstract concepts, motivating pupils to apply what they are learning to the world around them, for example why do you prefer the car driving on road then mud model of refraction, rather than the marching model of refraction?

Case study: Ethics in biology in Year 10, Joanne Crofts

Ethics can be a subject that some teachers dread teaching, due to the emotional links that students have to many of the topics discussed. Within biology, ethical topics come up often including:

- stem cells
- obesity and diabetes
- monoclonal antibodies
- cloning

- IVF treatment and embryo screening
- selective breeding and intensive farming methods.

Aesthetic questioning is a technique that encourages students to think about ethics in a logical and engaging way. An example of engaging students through the use of aesthetic questions might include:

- Providing several case studies of the topic being discussed, for example application forms from families applying for IVF.
- Adding societal context for ethical consideration, for example include applications from families from diverse backgrounds.
- Including financial pressures, for example only half of the applications can be accepted.
- Asking students to make decisions through the use of aesthetic questions, for example which family they would choose.

Then ask student the following questions:

- Why did you choose family A over family B?
- How do you think your choice would make family B feel?
- Would you change your mind if family B changed one of their lifestyle choices?
- What about those families who cannot so easily change their circumstances, for example due to health issues or their age?
- Family A has more money than family B, so should they fund their own IVF treatment?

Through the use of aesthetic questioning, students are motivated to learn more not only about ethics, but about thc decision making process and the scientific concept of IVF.

Joanne Crofts is a teacher of science at the Hart School, part of the Creative Education Trust. She tweets at @Miss_Crofts

Why should we explore new places and ideas?

Most of the ideas discussed so far develop epistemic curiosity, a thirst for deeper knowledge within the subject of study, and look at how it can affect motivation for learning. However diverse curiosity can also play a key part in the learning process.

When students are attracted to a concept that is new or novel, this is mostly down to diverse curiosity. Young children often ask questions such as 'Why? What's that? What about this? How does that work?' in quick succession. This may not lead to deep knowledge or a well-developed schema in a specific area, but can form the foundations of a wide base of prior knowledge which can then be built on methodically.

Exploring new places and ideas can require high levels of explicit instruction from teachers, and with careful planning can yield great benefits for a student's motivation in the long term. As shown in the psychological model of learning, with top-down processing some prior knowledge is needed to guide the sensory input. In many reception classrooms, teachers and teaching assistants guide pupils to build a wide schema through developing diverse curiosity.

How can we explore new places and ideas?

Techniques used to implement this include (but are not limited to):

- reading books on a wide variety of areas
- watching videos, including those on YouTube, around the topic being studied
- going on field trip to a local park or museum
- discussing the local context and the daily experiences of students in your setting
- discussing the daily experiences of students in other settings
- asking students what they did on their holiday or over the weekend.

Many of these ideas can be implemented within the curriculum time of a school day or set as activities for home learning. They help to form the hinterland of a pupil's understanding of a concept, very often bridging the gap between an abstract idea and a concrete experience from their daily lives.[16] In subjects where this wider knowledge of the curriculum is key, where pupils need to give their own opinion, we need to consider how we craft this breadth of knowledge and motivate students to learn around the subject.

It is crucial that these activities do not take away from the core learning that pupils are doing. This can be achieved by creating lists of suggested activities, reading lists, video playlists, local events and trips to encourage pupils to develop their wider understanding.

16. Counsell, C. (2018, April 7). Senior Curriculum Leadership 1: The indirect manifestation of knowledge: (A) curriculum as narrative [Blog post]. Retrieved from https://bit.ly/3fBa9lg

Exploring new places and ideas in action

- In **languages** to motivate students to learn more of a language by exposing them to the culture of a country through the use of pictures, books and films.
- In **computing** by visiting industry and places of work that use technology, to motivate students to learn about the variety of ways computer science affects the world around us.
- In **KS2** where a visit to a local landmark or a field trip to a park can motivate students to learn about a wide range of topics including plant and animal life, local history and statistical techniques.

Summary of Motivation

When considering the motivational ideas to encourage pupils to learn, I am reminded of a trip I took to *The Making of Harry Potter* with my wife and five-year-old daughter. We had just seen the Harry Potter films over the summer, and being fans of the series, decided we would like to go to the studios with my daughter. As we went around the tour, we asked our daughter questions about the films, big picture questions, reminding her of her knowledge of key aspects of the narrative in the movies. As she saw that the tour was sequenced in similar ways to the narrative of the films; the question 'What do you think we will see next?' was asked often. As part of the tour, we saw two aspects of how special effects were used in the movies; practical effects with the raising of a broomstick attached to a lift, and CGI where a green screen was used to simulate flying on a broomstick. Instantly my daughter noticed the difference between how the two worked. I asked her the aesthetic question 'Which did you like better, raising the broomstick or flying on the broomstick?' Her response sparked a conversation which still continues today whenever we watch a film; 'I liked the broomstick more, because I could see it all and could pretend better.' The conversation about practical effects versus CGI now comes about in every live action film we watch, and her love of practical effects motivated her and increased her interest in going to see musical theatre productions.

Motivation is arguably the key lever when driving engagement, and can be fostered using activities in the classroom. Through considering the ideas discussed, we can gain a better understanding of what motivates students to learn, and how we can affect it.

- Consider the use of big picture questions to frame carefully sequenced content, don't let the questions dictate the order of the content.

- Where causal links exist in content, consider the use of storytelling as a motivational technique.
- Ask questions that encourage pupils to consider their own opinions, which in turn motivates students to engage in the learning process.
- Encourage the development of diverse curiosity as well as epistemic, to ensure that pupils have a wide breadth of schema to build upon.

MARGE MODEL OF LEARNING: MOTIVATE: Develop curiosity, and a thirst for knowledge through developing a broad schema			
	What it is ...	Focus on ...	Be wary of ...
Big picture questions	Designing a lesson or a sequence of lessons to answer a question that covers a broad range of content.	Using questions that are open and inspire students. Allowing students to be guided through a topic within a subject as a process of answering an overarching question.	Using narrow questions with simple answers that do not show the breadth of the topic being covered. Using questions that are too broad, forcing links between topics that wouldn't naturally occur.
Harness storytelling	Sequencing the delivery of content to follow storytelling structures, using this as a motivational tool to inspire future learning.	Where possible include the ideas of causality, conflict, complications and character when delivering knowledge to foster motivation.	Shoehorning in a storytelling technique where it is not appropriate.
Aesthetic questions	Using questions to engage students' emotions and thoughts as part of the learning process.	Asking questions that engage a personal response from students to motivate them; Did you like that? Why did you find that easy to understand? What do you think about this topic?	Accepting the opinions of students over facts within the subject. The personal response should allow you to guide future learning rather than affect the value of what is being taught.
Exploring new places and new ideas	Developing students' diverse curiosity as well as their epistemic curiosity by broadening their experiences.	Directing students towards experiences and activities that are related directly to curriculum content.	Focussing solely on epistemic or diversity curiosity; both are present in highly motivated and engaged students who are keen to learn.

CHAPTER 2
A: ATTEND

Attention takes effort – it is an active process that requires conscious awareness of learning goals.[17]

Shimamura says:

You must attend to learn efficiently:[18]

- Get settled and be aware of what you want to learn.
- Chunk new information by actively grouping it into meaningful units.
- Categorise, compare and contrast to sustain attention.
- Take a guided tour by viewing learning as gathering information along a path of knowledge.
- Act as a student's PFC by facilitating executive control and top-down processing.

17. Shimamura, A. (2018), p18
18. Ibid.

In this chapter, these areas will be linked to the following strategies to encourage students to attend to the correct information while learning:

- Explicit learning goals.
- Chunking.
- Using the three Cs.
- Taking a guided tour.

Why do we need to focus our attention?

Motivation may be the starting point of the learning process, but students must direct this motivation and attend to the right information. From the moment pupils walk through the classroom door, they are taking in information from their environment; the conversations they are having with their friends, the smell of the room, what is written on the board, what is left on the tables from the previous lesson. The attention of students is up for grabs and it must be harnessed within the first few minutes if cognitively active learning is going to take place for the majority of the lesson.

We understand that learning is a top-down process, with knowledge informing what sensory information is attended to. With vast amounts of information being received at any one point in time, paying attention allows us to filter that information, ensuring that our focus is on information that links to what we already know and what we are trying to learn.

As I write this paragraph, I can hear a car drive by, the distant horn on a train, the rattling of the blinds as the breeze flows in through the open window, and feel the heat of the laptop keyboard; all of these are competing for my attention when the one thing I should be focussing on is 'what is attention; what do I know about it and how am I going to explain it?'

'Mind-wandering' is a common phenomenon in classrooms. Shimamura mentions that 'Classroom studies have shown that mind-wandering is rampant with only 40-46% of students paying attention to the lecturer at any given moment.'[19] This is an alarming statistic and demonstrates what teachers are up against when they haven't got the attention of the entire class, or when the class is not attending to the correct information. The first few minutes of a lesson are absolutely crucial for directing the attention of students. This settling in period can be effectively used to inform students:

19. Shimamura, A. (2018), p16

- what they are learning in the lesson today
- how today's learning will link to prior learning, including how it is similar and different to areas that have already been taught
- about an overview of what they will be expected to know within the curriculum, for learning from the lesson to be deemed successful.

In his paper *Learning: What is it, and how might we catalyse it?* Peps Mccrea discusses attention in two main ways: what we attend to is what we learn, and we can only attend to a few things at once.[20] He states that we should actively monitor and manage attention to ensure students focus on the right things and can therefore build useful mental models of the knowledge we are delivering. He also writes that students can only attend to limited information (two or three pieces) at any one time, and that we should therefore reduce the number of sources of information students are expected to use during instruction. If we consider the standard process of talking to a student about a new concept, that is one bit of information they need to attend to. If we are encouraging them to link this to prior knowledge, this is the second area of focus. For many students, this is the limit. If they are now trying to follow along with a picture in a textbook, or a presentation on the board, a third focus of their attention is added to the learning process. This could lead to their mind wandering as they have too many things to attend to and become cognitively overloaded.

The next challenge is maintaining attention once it has been secured. A simple example of disrupting attention within tasks is the 'split attention effect'[21] where students are asked to take in information in the same sensory mode, for example visual information from two different places on the same worksheet. A simple way around this would be to integrate the instructions within the diagram, so when producing methods for a science experiment, include the methods on the diagram, rather than putting them in a separate place on the same sheet.

Attention can also be disrupted when completing and switching between tasks. When switching between tasks, or methods of delivering knowledge, what we are actually doing is switching the focus of attention, and it is key that during these transitions attention is not lost. There are many strategies for ensuring this does not happen; variation in tone, gesturing towards key words or diagrams or warning students that a transition is about to occur. All these strategies rely on one thing: strategically using sensory input to direct attention.

20. Mccrea, P. (2018). *Learning what is it, and how might we catalyse it?* Retrieved from https://bit.ly/31LvgZT
21. Chandler, P. & Sweller, J. (1992). The split attention effect as a factor in the design of instruction. *British Journal of Educational Psychology*, 62(2), 233-246.

If motivation is opening the blinds to let the light in as part of the learning process, attention is using a lens to focus that light; attending to the most important information, comparing, contrasting and categorising it to link it to what is already known. Shimamura suggests four main techniques to improve the effectiveness of students' attention in the classroom:

1. **Explicit learning goals** – ask questions that make it clear what you are expecting students to be able to do by the end of the lesson.
2. **Chunking** – group information together into meaningful units that can be assimilated into students' existing schema.
3. **The three Cs** – categorise, compare and contrast ideas when first coming across them.
4. **Taking a guided tour** – use the model of being a tour guide to lead students through the curriculum, focussing their attention on key pieces of knowledge and the links between them.

Why should we use explicit learning goals?

When discussing motivational ideas in the previous chapter, the concept of a big picture question was used to show how students' interest in a subject can be grown by them seeing the big picture. Big picture questions are most useful when they are underpinned with clear structure and content, but on a lesson-by-lesson basis it may be difficult for a pupil to specifically pick out which part of the question they need to attend to, and therefore they may find it difficult to focus on what they already know about what is being taught. When students are about to start top-down processing, it is important they know exactly what prior knowledge they need to use to guide the next steps in their learning. Explicit learning goals get around this issue as they are a series of short, focussed questions that can be asked at the start and end of each lesson allowing students to focus their attention on what needs to be learned.

How can we use explicit learning goals?

Explicit learning goals can be made by breaking the big picture question down into a series of smaller questions. These questions should underpin the content that the big picture question is covering.

They can be used in lessons to allow students to:

- assess their own understanding
- activate prior knowledge

- pause and attend carefully to instruction when these areas are being discussed.

Explicit learning goals provide a framework of attention for students; 'What is it I need to know? How might I be asked about this? What do I need to check I can do at the end of the lesson?'

In the box below is an example of the big picture question from the *Motivate* chapter, broken down using explicit learning goals.

How are visible and invisible waves used by humans to improve the quality of life and how can they be dangerous?

- What are the two different types of wave?
- Which waves are visible, and which are invisible?
- How do each of these types of wave travel?
- What are the uses of sound waves, infrasound waves and ultrasound waves, and are they dangerous?
- Which waves form the electromagnetic spectrum?
- What are the properties of each of the waves in the electromagnetic spectrum?
- What are the uses and dangers of each of the waves in the electromagnetic spectrum?

It is important to remember that while these explicit learning goals are fixed goalposts that students are aiming at, the structure underneath them is fluid. Through expert questioning and scaffolding teachers can guide students towards these goals, correcting misconceptions, plugging gaps in knowledge, and responding to answers.

Explicit learning goals in action

- In **media** to break down a bigger question of 'What is the aim of a music video and how is this represented in the example provided?' into smaller, more manageable goals. For example, 'How do music videos, including the example provided, promote sales, promote new artists and promote the image of the artist?'
- In **history** where an explicit learning goal can be used to zoom in on larger parts of big picture questions. For example, 'How can historians solve the problem of identifying causality in conflict' can be broken

down into 'What were the causes of World War I? Which causes were long-term and which were short-term?'

- In **reception** explicit learning goals are written around students being able to talk about the shape and size of everyday objects, allowing staff and students to know what to focus their attention on, for example being able to order shapes from smallest to largest.

Why should we use chunking?

Shimamura discusses the need for learning to be presented in small 'chunks' of information that make it easier to process.

> *How can we sustain attention while learning? Top-down engagement is the key. We need to guide our thoughts and focus on relevant bits of information that add to our knowledge base. An important way to sustain attention is to chunk information – that is, group new information into meaningful units.*[22]

The chunks of new information have to be meaningfully connected as a single chunk, but also meaningfully connected to what is already known. As an example, if students were learning about different contact and non-contact forces, the information could be chunked so they were first taught a definition of contact forces and given a list of them, then a definition of non-contact forces and again provided with a list of examples. This allows students to easily process the contents of these lists and relate them to any existing schema, leading to more efficient learning taking place.

Much has been written in the past about presenting information in smaller subsets of the whole topic. In Barak Rosenshine's *Principles of Instruction: Research-Based Strategies That All Teachers Should Know* he explains that from his observations, smaller sets of information – and developing mastery of this content – is at the root of efficient learning.

> *The more successful teachers did not overwhelm their students by presenting too much new material at once. Rather, they presented only small amounts of new material at one time, and they taught in such a way that each point was mastered before the next point was introduced.*[23]

With what we know about top-down processing, and the need for the PFC to attend to the right external stimuli, presenting information in small steps

22. Shimamura, A. (2018), p1
23. Rosenshine, B. (2012). Principles of instruction: research-based strategies that all teachers should know. *American Educator*, 36(1), 12-19. Retrieved from https://www.aft.org/sites/default/files/periodicals/Rosenshine.pdf

makes sense. It ensures less information is being input and therefore processed, making it easier to decide on its relevance and establish links between incoming knowledge and what is already known.

How can we use chunking?

Chunking can be effectively used not only within a single lesson, but also across a sequence of lessons. After breaking down an idea into its constituent parts, these can then be grouped back together into meaningful chunks and sequenced coherently within a unit of work. Here is an example of a series of maths lessons where students are being taught how to represent data they have collected in the form of a graph.

Constructing a graph from raw data	Chunk 1	Define variables; independent, dependent, etc.
		Define different types of data; continuous, discrete, etc.
		Recognise different types of data; continuous, discrete, etc.
	Chunk 2	Define different types of charts and graphs
		Describe when we use each type of chart and graph
	Chunk 3	Design a results table to collect data
		Round data to the correct number of s.f or d.p
		Calculate the average of data
	Chunk 4	Construct scales for graphs
		Plot data onto graphs
		Construct lines of best fit
		Define and identify anomalies

The following process could be used to guide the process of chunking:

- Discuss the knowledge required to complete the larger aim, which in this case is constructing a graph.
- Break this down into its smallest constitute parts.
- Groups similar idea together into chunks.
- Sequence the chunks in an order with a clear rationale.

The chunking effect states that when we are repeatedly exposed to a chunk of knowledge, we assimilate it with related chunks, making one larger chunk which can be stored in long-term memory. Chunking work for our students allows us to free up their working memory, allowing them to attend more closely to the information we are providing.

Another useful method of chunking is discussed in Oliver Caviglioli's *Dual Coding with Teachers*[24] where he gives examples of three ways of using graphic organisers to chunk information:

- Tree diagrams
- Mind maps
- Concept maps

Tree Diagram

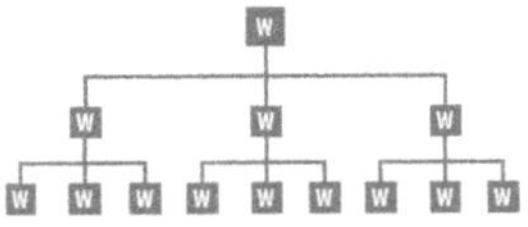

Mind Map

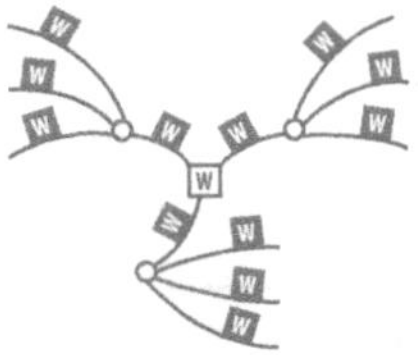

Concept Map

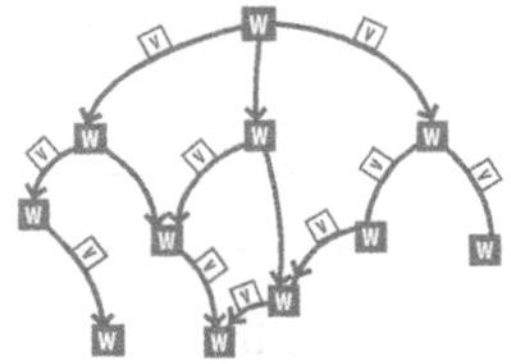

Tree diagrams are hierarchical and can be used to chunk information in a way that allows users to see how an overarching concept links to smaller parts. This helps focus students' attention by showing them the route to move through when learning new knowledge.

Mind maps work in the same way as a tree diagram, but spread out from a central point. This supports the attention of students in the same way as a tree diagram.

Concept maps follow a hierarchical structure and also include mini-sentences that allow links between concepts to be explained. This can help students who are struggling with attention by providing clear guidance to direct attention.

Each of these have their own benefits and drawbacks, and it is worth considering which would be best suited to direct the attention of your students, and which best supports the concept being delivered.

Chunking in action

- In **reception** and **KS1** when mapping the numeracy curriculum. For example, discussing each number in turn as a chunk, going through examples and non-examples, discussing common misconceptions, the number in terms of the number of sides on an object and also any number bonds that make it up.
- In **business** when delivering a lesson on the hierarchy of organisations and their structure. For example, going through each level of the organisation first, then considering departments.

24. Caviglioli, O. (2019). *Dual Coding for Teachers*. Woodbridge: John Catt. p50

- In **art** when teaching techniques that can be used in different types of painting. For example, chunking techniques that are often used in portrait painting separately from techniques used in still life painting.

Why should we use the three Cs to support attention?

Throughout his book, Shimamura, like many others who have studied the process of learning, states that the acquisition of new knowledge is based on integrating new information with what is already known. Using the three Cs he explains three ways in which knowledge can be handled to make it easier to integrate:

- Categorise – sorting knowledge into sets.
- Compare – looking for similarities between knowledge sets.
- Contrast – looking for differences between knowledge sets.

The three Cs will come up again in the Relate and Generate sections of this book, but for now we will discuss how the three Cs can be used to engage pupils' attention.

The key to attention for the purpose of learning is getting the PFC to draw on the right information from long-term memory. From the moment students engage at the start of a lesson, a large amount of information is going into their mind, ready to be processed. Not all of it is relevant; this where the three Cs can be used to support the process of gaining and maintaining attention.

How can we use the three Cs?

We can use an example from geography to help us understand a simple way to use the three Cs to focus attention. A list of keywords from the lesson could be put up on the board as pupils enter. Pupils could then compare and contrast them with what they already know, engaging with the process of activating prior knowledge. This could easily be done as a Think-Pair-Share activity. Give students an opportunity, preferably in silence, to think about the keywords within the framework of categorise, compare, and contrast. Allow them to discuss their ideas in pairs. Circulate the room and listen out for students saying things such as:

- solar panels are similar to when we learned about wind turbines, both are renewable energy sources
- I think non-renewable are the opposite of renewable fuels
- do you think fossil fuels and nuclear fuels are similar ideas, in that they are all non-renewable?

To further examine students' thinking and focus their attention on the key ideas being discussed, a set of follow-up questions could be:

- what makes you think solar panels and wind turbines are both renewable energy sources?
- how are non-renewable and renewable energy sources different?
- how are fossil fuels and nuclear fuels linked together?

By doing this, we encourage students to attend not only to the information we are delivering, but also to specific information from their long-term memory. Part of the key with the three Cs is the ability to give an example of an idea as part of your instruction, and also a non-example. By comparing and contrasting you can say what something is like, but also what it is not like.

The key to this process is that it allows students to attend to a concrete example in their own minds, allowing them to focus on processing the relevant new information.

The three Cs in action

- In **English** when **comparing** poems with similar themes but **contrasting** contexts. For example, the same theme of love and relationships but the contexts could be different historical time periods. After teaching the first poem, the teacher can say the second poem is a similar example to the first poem for the theme, but is a non-example for context, where they differ.
- In **maths** when teaching methods of solving equations, **contrasting** completing the square and substitution techniques, to show students how they differ. This will ensure students' attention is on the correct procedure.
- In **RE** when **categorising** and **comparing** the religious beliefs of different faiths and their geographical origins. For example, comparing thoughts on the afterlife in Buddhism and Hinduism.

Why should we use the concept of taking a guided tour?

In the previous chapter, I mentioned how my daughter was motivated to learn about how films were made – especially the special effects – by going on a guided tour of a movie studio set. Shimamura mentions how the model of a guided tour can be used to help students attend to the right information.

> *Construct lecture material as if it were a guided tour – note important points along the way and show how information is linked. At the end of a*

lecture, review the 'path' taken during class and how it fits in with previous (and future) lectures.[25]

The reason a tour guide manages to keep the attention of their party could be because they:

- have a clear plan, with relevant activities grouped together
- have explicit goals for what they want to achieve
- regularly ask aesthetic questions to check their party is motivated
- broaden the horizons of the people they are taking on a tour
- have a deep subject knowledge which they use to compare, contrast and categorise what they are talking about with the experiences of their party.

The tour guide model can be used with teachers when discussing their practice, as the links between having high levels of motivation and attention and using a tour guide model are clear. However, this is not a checklist, and simply by discussing this model with teachers you will not find a magic bullet to instantly motivate and gain the attention of all your students. It does, however, serve as a useful starting point for discussions with staff about potential strategies that can be implemented in the classroom.

How can we use the concept of taking a guided tour?

If we think of the knowledge within a subject as a map, then we as teachers need to navigate and communicate a path through this. Along this path there will be key pieces of knowledge we want students to attend to, and teachers can use the model in various ways:

- Signpost key knowledge and threshold concepts you wish students to attend to.
- Make the links explicit between new knowledge and what has already been learned.
- Share the narrative that links the knowledge together.
- Check for understanding before moving on to ensure nothing has been missed.
- Carefully sequence concepts, picking up where the last one left off.

These ideas direct students' attention and ensure that through a carefully crafted and sequenced set of events, long-term learning can happen. A good tour guide never lets a member of his party wander off course, in the same way a teacher prevents mind-wandering through focussing attention.

25. Shimamura, A. (2020, March 29). *Kids stuck at home?* Retrieved from https://bit.ly/3wtCj7C

Taking a guided tour in action

- In **science** when discussing the idea of surface area to volume ratio. For example, guiding students to its importance in areas such as organ adaptations within the body, or rates of reaction and diffusion.
- In **KS1** when teaching about Florence Nightingale in history, learning can be linked to themes from other subjects. For example, the idea of helping others from **PSHE**, an understanding of the relevant location of countries from **geography** and hygiene from **science**.
- In **sociology** taking students through a guided tour of their journey through school and education while linking this to ideas from sociology such as banding, streaming and the hidden curriculum.

Summary of Attend

Much of this chapter on A and the previous chapter on M, have discussed the idea of zooming out and zooming in to the knowledge a student holds in their memory, and what knowledge they are gaining in the lesson. Blake Harvard discusses this process in his blog *Zooming In and Zooming out.*[26] The idea of a camera lens is used to describe what students are attending to. When zoomed in, students can see the fine detail of their learning, the individual units that make up a subject. When zoomed out, students can see the links between each unit of information, and how the whole subject maps together. Students with a fixed lens are discussed as students without the knowledge to zoom in to see finer detail or zoom out to create links between sections of knowledge. Part of the skill of maintaining the attention of our students is choosing the right time to zoom in and out. Coherent curriculum planning is also vital, as a well planned curriculum will maintain attention.

When summing up this chapter I am reminded of the first two points discussed in the strategy from *Teach like a Champion*: progressing from unit planning to lesson planning, and using a well-framed objective to define the goal of each lesson.[27] These underpin the key considerations from this chapter for maintaining the attention of our students:

- Make what you are expecting to achieve explicitly clear to students.
- Break down the content into small manageable chunks to avoid mind-wandering.

26. Harvard, B. (2020). *Zooming in and out.* Retrieved from https://bit.ly/3cQLBCM
27. Lemov, D. (2015). *Teach Like a Champion 2.0.* San Francisco: Jossey-Bass. p56

- Categorise, compare and contrast knowledge you are going to deliver to ensure it does not confuse pupils, and make sure they know exactly what prior knowledge they need to be using at any moment in time.
- Consider the tour guide model when reflecting on how well you facilitate the attention of your students to key information.

MARGE MODEL OF LEARNING: ATTEND: Direct attention to engage in top-down processing			
	What it is ...	Focus on ...	Be wary of...
Explicit learning goals	Breaking down overarching themes or questions into the explicit goals that are required to be successful.	Creating a set of statements or questions that make it explicitly clear what students need to pay attention to within explanations.	Leaving the definition of success too vague within the topic, so students are unsure of what they need to be able to understand and do.
Chunking	Taking individual pieces of information and grouping them together into related 'chunks'. Breaking a process down into its smallest parts before relating them together.	Clearly pointing out the links between closely related pieces of knowledge, demonstrating how they are chunked. Breaking a process down into the individual steps that make it up, making it clear what pupils need to pay attention to.	Overcomplicating simple ideas or breaking a process down so far that it is no longer recognisable as part of the overarching theme.
The three Cs	Using the ideas of comparing, contrasting and categorisation to direct students' attention towards links between new and existing knowledge.	Using the three Cs in a clear way, directing students' attention to exactly what you want them to compare, contrast or categorise.	Being vague when defining the terms compare, contrast and categorise, in case students cannot tell the difference between them.
Taking a guided tour	Considering the knowledge within a subject as a map, with your role as a teacher to act as a tour guide through it.	Having a clear plan of your route through a topic, so there is a clear sequence to learning, allowing you to signpost key content.	Hopping between 'sites' of key knowledge, not considering the sequences in which the knowledge is covered.

CHAPTER 3
R: RELATE

Chapter written by Dawn Ashbolt

Relate it to make it stick![28]

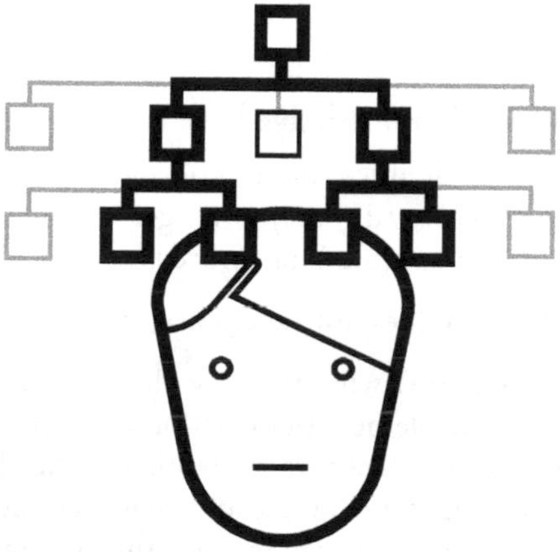

Shimamura says:

Relate new information to existing knowledge:[29]

- Chunk knowledge into meaningful units.
- Associate areas of knowledge through considering the use of acronyms, verbal mediators and visual imagery.
- Use the three Cs to think about the links between knowledge.
- Integrate knowledge by applying elaborative interrogation and mental movies.
- Relate knowledge by using metaphors and analogies to link new concepts to prior knowledge.
- Organise knowledge through the use of schematic representations.

28. Shimamura, A. (2018), p27
29. Ibid.

Within this chapter, these areas will be linked to the following strategies to encourage students to relate knowledge to prior learning, leading to long-term learning:

- Mnemonics to relate concepts.
- Mental movies, metaphors and analogies.
- Schematic representations.
- Applying the three Cs.

Note: strategies discussing chunking in the three Cs and elaborative interrogation are also discussed in the Attend and Generate chapters.

Why do we need to relate knowledge?

Relate within MARGE is all about the importance of securing memory. The new information we teach every day may never get beyond the working memory of our students, so will not be stored for future use.

If memory consolidation does not take place, then neither does learning!

The question that Shimamura's work poses is: How do we support the teaching and learning process to enable new information to be securely stored? This is what we all want and need as teachers. How many times have you thought to yourself after marking a set of mocks 'I know I have taught this, so why haven't they got the answer right?' or 'How can they get this wrong? I only taught it last week?' The answer lies in understanding that teaching something doesn't mean students have learned it. To enable learning, information needs to be repeated and presented clearly, preferably via a range of techniques.

Shimamura strongly argues that the ideal place to begin the learning process is by relating the new information you are teaching to what students already know. New information needs connecting to what is already in place in the schema of your students. In this respect, prior knowledge is an important factor in enabling our brain to store any new information. He references a memory study where individuals in two groups were tasked to learn a set of 18 minerals.[30] One group was shown just the words in a random presentation and asked to remember them. The other group was shown not just the words but a diagram representing them within a conceptual hierarchy, grouped into meaningful sub-categories such as metals and stones. The results were impressive and showed that the group remembering the random words

30. Shimamura, A. (2018), p24

only retained 18% of the words compared to 65% for the group where links were made. This demonstrates the power of relating groups of knowledge.

Shimamura goes on to discuss note-taking during lessons, saying that it should be structured using a hierarchical outline to show relational links. Students can find taking notes difficult as it involves being able to listen, process and write down key information quickly and accurately. When he lectures, he provides students with partial outlines of his lecture notes which include the main headings and sub-headings of the topics to be covered. The students then have a structure to follow and can add their own notes under the headings, linking what they are learning to what they already know.

Shimamura suggests four main techniques to improve the effectiveness of students' ability to relate prior knowledge to new knowledge in the classroom:

1. **Mnemonics** – these allows students to remember key facts by linking them to prior knowledge in related chunks.
2. **Mental movies, metaphors and analogies** – to allow what is being learned to be linked to what is already known.
3. **Schematic representations** – to clearly demonstrate the links between areas of knowledge.
4. **Applying the three Cs** – developing the links between areas of knowledge by comparing, contrasting and categorising them.

Why should we use mnemonics?

In the classroom, the memorisation of often quite large amounts of information is an absolute necessity, while in the real world, it has become increasingly redundant. Hattie considers the contemporary world that we live in and how our need to memorise information and large banks of data has decreased over time.[31] Key bits of data, such as phone numbers and bank details, are now generally saved on devices and not in our brains. Given this reduction in the requirement for memorisation (and, as a result, the decline in our practice of performing it), Hattie suggests there is a need to develop powerful mnemonic skills in the classroom to train students' memories. He argues that mnemonics offer teachers clear techniques to support memorisation in students, especially when the memory load is high.

Some new knowledge, a list of dates or names for example, may not relate to anything a student already has in their consolidated memory. Then, Shimamura suggests, we should create new associations to force our brains into adding this

31. Hattie, J. (2013). *Visible learning and the science of how we learn*. Abingdon: Routledge. p168

new material to our consolidated memories. Mnemonics, both verbal and visual, are a good way to do this, making them an excellent technique to aid memory.

How can we use mnemonics?

There are various tools, such as a verse, song or word, which can be linked to new information to form a lasting association, so when the mnemonic is recalled, it sparks the memory of the related knowledge, helping in its retention and recollection.

The word mnemonic can be quite off-putting in itself, due to the silent 'm' at the start, but as it comes from the Greek word meaning 'to remember', it might be useful to link the *mem* of *memory* with the *mnem* of *mnemonics*, forming an association which reminds us that mnemonics is to do with memory, and vice versa. It is important to remember that mnemonics help us associate knowledge that can appear meaningless (as it does not associate with what we already know) to meaningful knowledge we have already stored. The table below contains different types of mnemonics that can be used to aid memory in the classroom, each of which has their own benefits and drawbacks to consider.[32]

Musical or song	Remembering knowledge to a tune or a jingle that you already know, for example children remember the alphabet by singing the ABC song.
Name (acronym)	The first letter of each word is put together to make a new word that is easier to remember, for example OILRIG for oxidation is loss, reduction gain.
Word or expression	The first letter of each word is combined to form a new sentence, for example Elephants And Donkeys Grow Big Ears for EADGBE, the tuning of a guitar.
Method of loci	Link locations that you are familiar with to the knowledge you need to remember, for example associating planets with rooms on a corridor can help you remember the order of planets in the solar system.
Peg word or rhyme	Memorise knowledge by linking it to words that rhyme with key words in it. Visualise the rhyming word for the place in the order with the order the knowledge is required, for example one rhymes with bun, two rhymes with shoe, three rhymes with tree. If the order of knowledge goes red, green, yellow then this can be remembered using red bun, green shoe and yellow tree.
Visual	Store the information within a picture or piece of visual imagery, for example remembering which months have 31 days by using your knuckles.
Link	Visualise each bit of knowledge as connected to each other, for example to remember Venus is hot, high in CO_2 and low in water vapour you could visualise a cartoon planet of venus, sweating, holding a glass containing little water, and a canister of CO_2.
First letter	Take the first letter of the knowledge to be learned and use that to create a new sentence that is easier to remember, for example to remember Domain, Kingdom, Phylum, Class, Order, Family, Genus, Species it can be put into the sentence Dear King Philip Came Over For Good Soup.

32. Adapted from Willingham, D. T. (2010). *Why Don't Students Like School?* San Francisco: Jossey Bass. p77

Mnemonics in action

- In **KS2 science** to help remember the seven life processes: MRS NERG, Movement, Reproduction, Sensitivity, Nutrition, Excretion, Respiration, Growth.
- In **English** to help remember literary techniques: AFOREST, Alliteration, Fact, Opinion, Repetition or Rhetorical, Emotive, Statistics and Triples.
- In **history** when discussing the road to WW2; Roger Rabbit Always Sucks Carrots Politely for Rearmament, Rhineland, Anschluss, Sudetenland, Czechoslovakia, Poland.

Why should we use mental movies, metaphors and analogies?

The famous expression 'a picture is worth a thousand words' refers to the notion that complex information can be conveyed with just the use of a picture rather than with a written description. In this instance, the picture is a mental picture, created to support the recall of newly learned information.

Creating a mental movie, or even just an image, is a visualisation strategy that helps to reactivate and integrate new facts. If we consider why films are so popular and memorable with audiences, much of this is related to our ability to relate knowledge from visual imagery.

Metaphors and analogies can also help us make sense of new information by forging connections to something we already know. For example, early automobiles made sense to people because they were described as 'horseless carriages'.

A metaphor is a figure of speech that directly compares one thing to another for an effect. A great example of a metaphor is in William Shakespeare's *As You Like It*, where he writes 'All the world's a stage, and all the men and women merely players.' This is a great example of a metaphor. Shakespeare is comparing the world to a stage by saying one is the other, but he does not mean this in a literal sense. The comparison is rhetorical. By comparing the world to a stage, and the people in the world as players on it, he is making us all compare the similarities between these two things, linking to the three Cs, and the meaning of human nature and our place in the world.

An analogy serves a similar purpose as a literary technique, in that it is showing how two things are alike. The purpose of an analogy is not just to show, but also to explain in more detail, which is where the difference lies. A good example of this is if you consider this analogy for the concept of futility: 'What you're doing is as useful as rearranging deck chairs on the Titanic.'

Here, the person speaking is comparing the task being done to the job of rearranging deck chairs on the Titanic. The goal in using this analogy is not to compare one task to another, which is the main purpose of a metaphor, rather it is to communicate that the first task is useless, by comparing it to a similarly useless task, such as rearranging deck chairs on the Titanic as it sinks.

If difficult concepts are made clearer, it will help to support understanding through connecting new schemas to familiar ones.

How can we use mental movies, metaphors and analogies?

We can guide students through the process of making their own mental movie. They can start the process off by narrating the movie in their heads. By using new information and reformatting it into visual imagery, they are helping the brain to organise and retain it.

Some ideas that can help to make the mental movie more memorable include:

- using senses; sight, sound, smell, touch and taste
- making it colourful
- exaggerating and therefore making it exciting
- adding humour
- using a clear structure, for example once upon a time...
- adding emotion.

As with most new techniques in the classroom, you could start off by making a mental movie as a group, getting students to add in each next part as the movie progresses. Practice will be an important part of this technique if it is to be impactful on student learning.

Questions could be posed to guide the process:

- Where does the story begin?
- What can you see?
- What can you hear?
- What happens next? And why?

Metaphors and analogies can be used in all subjects to connect new knowledge to previously learned information. It's often considered a key tool in English lessons, but it could also be used across the curriculum. It is important to remind students that metaphors and analogies are a model of the situation being explained, and not the situation itself. It is also worth remembering that some SEND students may have difficulty in understanding abstract language and metaphors. Teaching the meaning of metaphors to students can sometimes help with their understanding of these concepts, but the need to be specific here is important so they don't feel confused.

Mental movies, metaphors and analogies in action

- In **KS1** when describing the life cycle of a plant through the use of analogies.
- In **science** when using a metaphor is used to describe abstract concepts such as white blood cells' role in the immune system, or to compare the size of a nucleus to its atom.
- In **geography** to make a mental movie of the processes involved in deforestation.

Why should we use schematic representations?

There are a range of benefits of using schematic representations. Ruth Clark and Chopeta Lyons' book *Graphics for Learning* emphasises how words and graphics are two basic tools that help learners build new knowledge and skills. They discuss how we generally have greater expertise with words as our early years education is focussed on the importance of reading and writing, but that the use and interpretation of graphics is a neglected skill.[33] While this chapter will focus on how graphics can be used to help relate knowledge and build long lasting memories, it is useful to look at all of MARGE when discussing the six reasons outlined by Clark and Lyons for how graphics can benefit students:

- **Graphics help to direct attention.** This links to the Attend concept within MARGE. The visual will help to attract attention but can cause distraction, so be careful. You need to make sure that the visual is relevant and not too complex. Simple visuals are more effective for novice learners.
- **Graphics help to activate prior knowledge.** The importance here is on bringing to the surface, and connecting with, relevant prior knowledge that students may have. This is key to the Relate concept within MARGE.
- **Graphics help to manage mental load.** Simple visuals are thought to be more effective than more complex visuals. As students become more competent with the content being taught, then the visuals can increase in their complexity. Making graphics lighter on mental load will free up greater mental capacity to make relational links between knowledge.

33. Clark, R. & Lyons, C. (2004). *Graphics for learning: proven guidelines for planning, designing, and evaluating visuals in training materials.* Hoboken, NJ: Pfeiffer. p3

- **Graphics help to build mental models/schema.** We all learn by relating new information to existing knowledge, which is Shimamura's mantra in MARGE. By using graphics, abstract information can become more concrete and clearer by showing how it links to current knowledge.
- **Graphics help with transfer.** Clark and Lyons argue that the important part in learning is being able to transfer knowledge to other situations.
- **Graphics can optimise motivation.** Clark and Lyons recommend using visuals that help learners see the value in the learning and develop their interest. This links with the Motivate concept in MARGE.

It is important to note that when using schematic or graphical representations, they do not draw attention away from the key core content. Materials that do this are often called seductive details:

> *Seductive details can be text, images, audio, gifs, memes, animations – anything that is tangentially related to the content, interesting, and irrelevant to the learning objective. The seductive details effect refers to the phenomenon where learners learn worse when seductive details are included than when they are excluded.* [34]

It has been shown that if this tangential, irrelevant knowledge forms the focus of students' attention, then they are less likely to perform well on learning tests.

How can we use schematic representations?

A conceptual hierarchy organises information into categories, and shows how those categories are related to each other, with sub-groups indicated beneath categories.

This helps students to remember and relate information more easily, as by defining a clear structure, they are more easily able to recall items from a particular category. In the example below, a student might more readily remember that swimming is an individual sport because of its position as one of three examples in that category in the conceptual hierarchy.

Sport	
Team	**Individual**
Netball	Tennis
Rugby	Long jump
Football	Boxing

34. Sundar, K. (2019). *Cut it out: learning with seductive details.* Retrieved from https://bit.ly/3wupPg8

Concept maps involve grouping and linking information in an image to show how concepts are related to each other. They help to organise ideas and support learning through a visual representation. They are different from conceptual hierarchies because the resulting diagram doesn't focus on hierarchies, but connections.

Shimamura uses this example from a geography topic. It provides the students with a visual schema, as Shimamura calls it, which will help them to define the relationships between each of the concepts or ideas.[35]

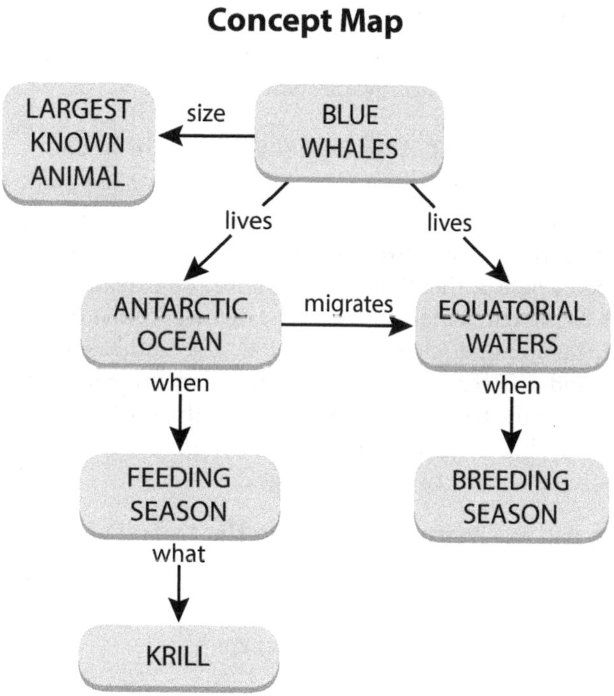
Concept Map
LARGEST KNOWN ANIMAL
size
BLUE WHALES
lives
lives
ANTARCTIC OCEAN
migrates
EQUATORIAL WATERS
when
when
FEEDING SEASON
BREEDING SEASON
what
KRILL

This concept map shows a clear way of representing how knowledge about whales, oceans, feeding and migration can be linked together. Shimamura offers a word of warning when using concept maps and conceptual hierarchy: you need to limit the number of links (arrows or subcategories) to no more than five for optimum use.

35. Shimamura, A. (2018), p25

The advantages are clear:

- Information can be represented visually.
- The links and connections can be seen with clarity.
- It will support recall in the same way that mental movies will.
- They help to clarify and structure ideas.

Schematic representations in action

- In **PSHE** to show the mental and physical benefits of an active lifestyle.
- In **history** to demonstrate hierarchy, timelines and sequences of events.
- In **drama** to demonstrate the links between the themes within a play, and how they are represented by different characters.

Why should we use the concept of applying the three Cs?

Shimamura argues that an effective way to integrate facts and concepts into existing knowledge frameworks is through the use of the three Cs – categorise, compare and contrast. These three Cs would fit perfectly within activities at the start of a lesson where, rather than launching into an explanation of a new topic and its links to the curriculum and exam structure, you start with getting the students to bring to mind related information. Ask students to find similarities (comparing) and differences (contrasting) between the new material that you are introducing in the lesson and what they may already know about that term, word, image or idea. Applying the three Cs is therefore crucial in terms of forming relational links between knowledge.

How can we use the concept of applying the three Cs?

Through applying the concept of the three Cs, students are forced to think about the knowledge they are taking in. This drives the process of relating what they are being taught to what is already known.

- By comparing different areas of knowledge students can see how they are similar, and therefore understand how knowledge structures within different areas may be built in similar ways.
- By contrasting different areas of knowledge, students can see how they are different and avoid relating knowledge together that should not have direct relational links.
- By categorising different areas of knowledge, students group them together, making it easier to relate them.

As Shimamura succinctly quotes in MARGE:

> *When you apply the three Cs, you actively attend to relevant features, reactivate the information, and relate it to your existing knowledge base.*[36]

In his book *Dual Coding with Teachers*,[37] Oliver Caviglioli uses these three diagrams when discussing comparing differing sets of knowledge in the form of graphic organisers. This usefully links the ideas of applying the three Cs and using schematic representations.

Venn Diagram

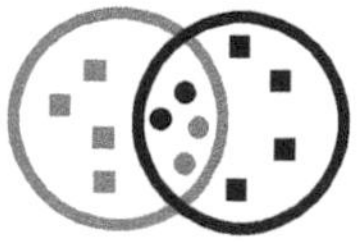

Venn diagrams are used to show how similar ideas within a topic can be grouped together (in the overlap) while differing ideas are kept apart within their individual circles.

Double Spray

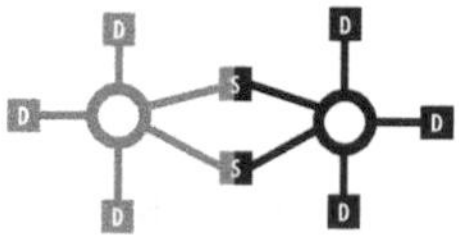
D
S
D
S
D
D
D
D

Double Spray diagrams are similar to Venn diagrams, where ideas in the centre contain similarities. They can be more useful than a Venn diagram when there are a set number of answers you want from a student.

Crossed Continua

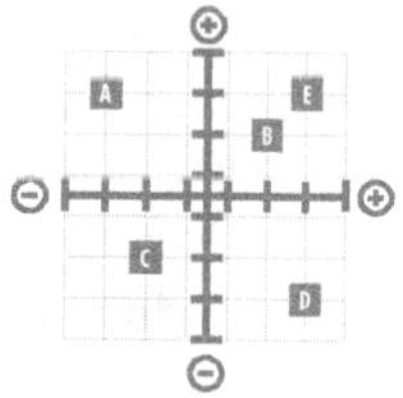
A
E
B
C
D

Crossed Continua diagrams can be used to compare two or more topics against two sets of criteria each on an axis or continuum. This allows comparisons and contrasts to be made depending on where points are plotted. Similar ideas fall close to each other, and quadrants can be categorised.

Applying the three Cs in action

- In **English** where a crossed contina can be used to plot different characters on the axes of helpfulness versus importance to the text. This can help with students' understanding of individual characters and their overall role in driving the narrative.
- In **media** where the features of specific genres of film can be compared for similarities and differences.
- In **KS2 geography** where students can compare, contrast and categorise different habitats from around the world.

36. Shimamura, A. (2018), p23
37. Caviglioli, O. (2019). *Dual Coding for Teachers.* Woodbridge: John Catt. p50

Summary of Relate

The premise of Relate as a concept within the MARGE model of learning is clear; when students start to make connections between new information and information already stored in their memory, they are reactivating that information, relating it to what they already know and, consequently, adding it to their long-term memory. Through applying the strategies highlighted in this chapter and the next, we are facilitating memory consolidation and long-term retention through elaboration and reactivation.

When summing up this chapter, it is important to remember that many of the techniques in the Relate section of MARGE are techniques to support relational memory, which is the ability to remember associations between objects or events. The key areas of the Relate section of MARGE are:

- Consider using mnemonics to help students remember arbitrary facts where the meaning of them may, at first, not be apparent.
- Consider using visual and verbal mediators, such as mental movies, metaphors and analogies to help build links between what is being taught and what is already known.
- Use schematic diagrams such as concept maps or conceptual hierarchies, to help show the links between areas of knowledge, and help organise student learning.
- Applying the three Cs to lesson structures allows students to reactivate what is already known and helps build upon it to create rich, well-developed schemas.

MARGE MODEL OF LEARNING: RELATE: Establish meaningful chunks of new information and relate them to existing knowledge			
	What it is ...	Focus on ...	Be wary of ...
Mnemonics to relate concepts	Using a variety of different techniques to memorise a number of facts that are required to unlock further understanding of concepts.	Using this as a technique to help students remember information that may not be directly related to anything already consolidated in their memory.	Students not understanding why they are being taught, what they are being taught; explain that while the relevance of what they are currently being taught may not be clear, it forms the basis of future learning.
Mental movies, metaphors and analogies	Explaining ideas using visual imagery or metaphors and analogies to help students integrate and reactivate facts.	Relating ideas to students' daily experiences and using metaphors and analogies for ideas they would have come across.	Distinguishing between the concept and the metaphor/analogy; explicitly explain that the metaphor/analogy is a model for the concept, not the actual concept itself.
Schematic representations	Using words and graphics to represent knowledge in a different format. This includes many ideas covered by the areas of graphic organisers.	Showing the links and categories within the knowledge being taught; how areas link together but also what makes them separate.	Over-complicating schematics, making text that was already difficult to understand into a more complex representation.
Applying the three Cs	Applying the principles of comparing, contrasting and categorising to newly learned knowledge.	Using the three Cs to encourage students to make relational links between areas of knowledge, potentially through the use of dual coding.	Trying to apply the three Cs to areas of knowledge that are too far apart, or where only non-relevant relational links would be formed.

CHAPTER 4
G: GENERATE

The key to long-lasting memories is the reactivation and elaboration of pertinent information after initial learning.[38]

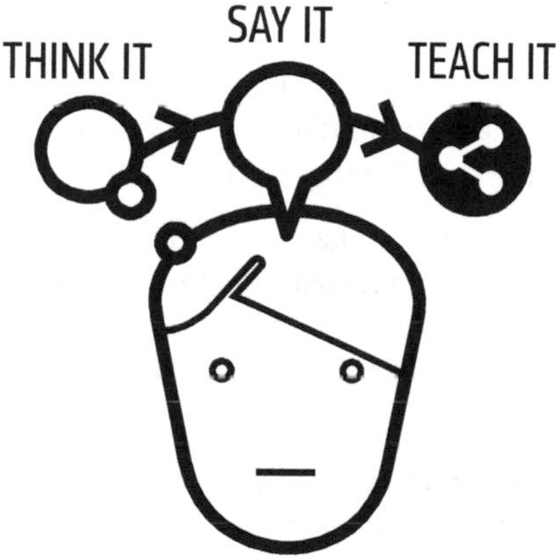
THINK IT
SAY IT
TEACH IT

Shimamura says:

Think it, say it, teach it:[39]

- Tell others about what you've learned, or rehearse it to yourself.
- Practice retrieving information in your own words.
- Test yourself using the three Cs, elaborative interrogation and schematic organisations.
- Space your retrieval practice.
- Teach material to others.

38. Shimamura, A. (2018), p30
39. Ibid.

Within this chapter, these areas will be linked to the following strategies to encourage students to generate knowledge as part of long-term learning:

- Telling others what you know through elaboration.
- The generation effect and the production effect.
- Self-testing using the three Cs.
- Spaced practice.

Why do we need to generate new learning?

Storing knowledge in long-term memory is one of the end goals of the learning process, along with ensuring that this knowledge is meaningful and can be applied in a variety of scenarios. Through the process of self-generating information in working memory, students can reframe what they have learned, putting it into their own words, leading to it becoming better established.

The ability to self-generate material has been linked by Shimamura to the ideas of practice and retrieval. He argues that by telling other people what you know in your own words, testing yourself using the idea of the three Cs, practicing elaborative interrogation and spacing out retrieval practice, you are more likely to consolidate memories.

> *To retain your conceptual knowledge well past the end of the academic year, you must work to re-activate it – use it or lose it.*[40]

This process of reactivation of knowledge must happen often in order for us to maintain strong links to long-term memories, and avoid forgetting, so reviewing knowledge at regular intervals increases the likelihood of it being retained. This theory was first proposed by Hermann Ebbinghaus in 1883[41] and has been verified in more recent studies.

However, just because you have not forgotten knowledge, that does not mean it is still meaningful to you and can be applied in a variety of situations. Knowledge we have learned must be able to be retrieved, then explained or applied. Efrat Furst discusses the four stages of memory processing in her excellent blog, *Reconsolidation: The 'life' of a memory trace.*[42]

40. Shimamura, A. (2018), p37
41. Ebbinghaus, H. (2013). Memory: a contribution to experimental psychology. *Annals of neurosciences*, 20(4), 155-156. Retrieved from https://doi.org/10.5214/ans.0972.7531.200408
42. Furst, E. (2018). *Reconsolidation. The life of a memory trace.* Retrieved from https://bit.ly/2QYvkDp

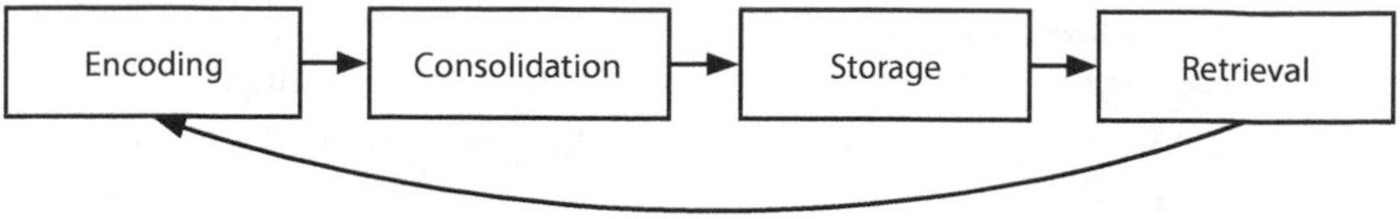
Encoding
Consolidation
Storage
Retrieval

Encoding – incoming information is processed using prior knowledge as a guide, which is linked to top-down processing. We give meaning to this new idea by having it linked to known ideas.

Consolidation – continues after the encoding process through thinking about what we are encoding. This leads to understanding the new idea through stabilising the encoding.

Storage – the information is now a memory, stored and inactive, no longer needed in working memory.

Retrieval – where external information triggers a process to reactivate stored knowledge that has a link to this new external information. This leads back to the start of the process, allowing new information to be encoded.

This links to the idea of self-generating material, and Shimamura's Generate principle. Students need to constantly use and reframe the knowledge they have, not just regurgitate facts verbatim, in order to improve their chance of remembering information and applying it successfully.

As stated in the last chapter, there are times when we need students to remember a list of facts, and where mnemonics can be used to aid memorisation. Through students understanding the role of these facts in future learning, the facts gain meaning. Returning to the example of the electromagnetic spectrum, if I gave students a list of the electromagnetic waves to remember, they might remember them in order using a mnemonic. They know they are electromagnetic waves, but there is no further meaning to them. If we then discuss that we will learn about the uses and dangers of these waves, the students begin to attach meaning to the names of the waves and can talk about them using their own language, reframing their understanding and generating stronger links in their schema.

The main purpose of this chapter is to discuss ways in which students generate new knowledge and reframe their understanding by consistently using what they know to ensure it is not forgotten and can be applied successfully. Shimamura suggests four main strategies for encouraging this process:

1. **Telling others what you know** – engage in the process of elaborative interrogation, expressing your thoughts and understanding.
2. **Consider the generation effect and the production effect** – reframe your knowledge in different ways to create new links.
3. **Self-testing using the three Cs** – testing yourself on knowledge that you should have (this could be done using the three Cs as a model).
4. **Spaced practice** – test yourself at intervals to suppress the effect demonstrated by the Ebbinghaus forgetting curve, as discussed later in this chapter.

Why should we use the concept of telling others what you know?

Elaboration has the potential to be a powerful learning technique:

> *One of the most potent manipulations that can be performed in terms of increasing a subject's memory for material is to have the subject elaborate on the to-be-remembered material.*[43]

At its core, elaboration is about adding knowledge to existing knowledge, which we have identified as being key to the learning process. It also allows learners to reactivate, reshape and reuse their knowledge by putting it into their own words.

Elaborative interrogation involves students being asked 'how' or 'why' questions about their understanding of material, which can lead to problems if the information being drawn together is incorrect. It is therefore crucial that when engaging in any of these types of processes, answers are checked for accuracy often.

Quite often in parents' evening conversations, the topic of how much students discuss their learning at home comes up. More often than not, parents would respond with the same answer, along the lines of 'All I ever get from my son/daughter is "nothing" or "I dunno"'. While this is frustrating for parents, it should also be frustrating for teachers. Through the sheer act of telling someone else what you know about a topic you are reinforcing knowledge and creating stronger links. One of the things I have noted during my time in education is that primary schools are exceptionally good at sharing with parents what is being learned about at school that can be discussed around the dinner table at home. As a secondary practitioner,

43. Postman, L. (1976). Methodology in human learning. In W. K. Estes (Ed.) *Handbook of Learning and Cognitive Processes, Volume 3: Approaches to Human Learning and Motivation*. Hove: Psychology Press.

I noted this and came up with simple ways of ensuring my own subject was represented at these dinner table discussions, through the idea of a five-a-day challenge sheet.

How can we use the concept of telling others what you know?

Many students use group chat conversations full of revision voice notes; recordings they send to each other where they elaborate on key ideas they have learned. The ideas discussed in these conversations can be steered by providing students with a list of topics to discuss and a set of high-quality revision notes around that topic. A 'five-a-day challenge sheet' is an example of a way these conversations can be guided.

The table below shows an example of a list of topics that could be discussed, on Monday of week one. A resource could then be populated with a list of five topics to be covered daily, over a period of weeks.

	Week 1
Monday	1. Distance-time graph
	2. Velocity-time graph
	3. Motion equations
	4. Newton's 1st Law
	5. Newton's 2nd Law

The key here is the types of questions that students ask themselves, or get others to ask them. Answers to questions could then be checked against revision notes to ensure they are accurate.

The five-a-day challenge topics can allow conversations at the dinner table to be guided by what students need to know, either to consolidate learning or prepare for assessment. They can also be used by students to guide topics they are elaborating on in their own revision groups.

Asking questions such as 'Why? How? What happens next?' encourages deeper thinking and looking for connections between units of knowledge. Dr Yana Weinstein demonstrates an excellent example of using these styles of questions around a picture of an aircraft:

> *How does a plane take off? Why does a plane need an engine? How does the upward lift force work?*[44]

44. Weinstein, Y., Madam, C., & Sumeracki, M. (2018). Teaching the science of learning. *Cognitive Research: Principles and Implications*, 3(2) Retrieved from https://bit.ly/3mu5Z00

Elaboration is crucial in engaging top-down processing, as students are using what they already know about an area to guide themselves in their acquisition of new knowledge.

Telling others what you know in action

- In **reception** to encourage students to explain about why objects fall over when they are constructing things, or to explain why they have grouped items in a certain way.
- In **RE** where students could justify their thoughts at the end of a lesson or a topic of work by using their factual knowledge in a debate.
- In **art** where students could be asked why they have made the choices they have, or how they have created a piece of work in a certain way.

Why should we use the generation effect and the production effect?

The generation effect has been observed in experiments where participants have demonstrated greater memory strength if they are asked to generate a response during encoding rather than just being provided with one. Shimamura discusses how he investigated this idea in his paper *The generation effect: activating broad neural circuits during memory encoding.*

> *The generation effect is a robust memory phenomenon in which actively producing material during encoding acts to improve later memory performance. In an fMRI analysis, we explored the neural basis of this effect. During encoding, participants generated synonyms from word-fragment cues (e.g. GARBAGE-W_ST_) or read other synonym pairs (e.g. GARBAGE-WASTE). Compared to simply reading target words, generating target words significantly improved later recognition memory performance.*[45]

Word fragment cues are when a section of a word is presented to help students deduce the rest of it. This works well when the word that is cued is linked to a similar word, such as in the example above.

The generation effect clearly has an impact when consolidating existing information and creating strong links within memory. Using the example above, the participant would have needed to know the word *waste* to be able to make the link with *garbage*. This suggests that memory strategies that depend

45. Rosner, Z., Elman, J., & Shimamura, A. (2013). The generation effect: activating broad neural circuits during memory encoding. *Cortex*, 49(7), 1901-1909. Retrieved from https://bit.ly/2PFFBEd

on the generation effect will have limited effectiveness when they are applied to new or unfamiliar material.

When investigating strategies for ideas that were less complex, the generation effect produces better testing results. Shimamura suggests that when the materials are simple – because there are few interacting elements or it has already been incorporated into long-term memory – learners should practice generating responses rather than being shown them.

The production effect states that if you 'do something' with newly acquired knowledge instantly, you are less likely to forget it. If pupils apply new learning right away they are less likely to get distracted and more likely to encode the learning into what is already known, therefore increasing its likelihood of being stored in long-term memory.[46] Newly acquired information should be used instantly, making it easier to encode.

How can we use the generation effect and the production effect?

When teachers talk through diagrams with students, they can use the generation effect to maximise long-term learning. Studies have shown that students are more likely to remember words attached to a picture if they have to generate the words from a cue,[47] which could be as simple as a scrambled-up word, or the first letter in a word. This idea could be used when providing a list of definitions for words and then presenting students with a diagram; students would need to place the defined words onto the diagram in the correct place. By getting students to use their newly acquired knowledge instantly, they are more likely to remember it in the long term. The same can be said for students testing themselves on what they just learned.

The generation effect and the production effect in action

- In **food and nutrition** when students are labelling diagrams and being questioned on the definitions of parts of the diagram, for instance cooking devices and utensils.
- In **KS2** when students are discussing an idea they can generate a list of features and relevant questions, for example 'What is the skin like? Does it have fur? Does it produce milk?' to produce a list of the features of a vertebrate.

46. Klemm, W. (2017, December 15). *Enhance memory with the 'production effect'*. Retrieved from https://bit.ly/3sV7OW1
47. Zormpa, E., Brehm, L., Hoedemaker, R., & Meyer, A. (2018). The production effect and the generation effect improve memory in picture naming. *Memory*, 27(3), 340-352. Retrieved from https://doi.org/10.1080/09658211.2018.1510966

- In **languages** where students apply the rules they have learned about tenses to generate past and future tense version of words, and then use them within a conversation.

Why should we use self-testing using the three Cs?

Self-testing can be framed using the idea of the three Cs of compare, contrast and categorise. Students can apply the three Cs to knowledge they have already gained, with guidance from a teacher. This allows the generation of links between areas of knowledge, allowing students to be more fluent when talking about their learning. This allows students to generate new knowledge by forming links between what is known.

It is important to separate the *generative* process involved in self-testing using the three Cs that will be covered in this chapter, from the evaluative features of self-quizzing that will be discussed in the *Evaluate* chapter.

The idea of applying the three Cs in a self-testing format is a powerful way to get students to prepare themselves to develop their knowledge of an area. For example, when looking at plate tectonics in geography they could ask themselves:

- How are the plate boundaries similar?
- How are the plate boundaries different?
- What defines each type of plate boundary from the others?
- How can I categorise the plate boundaries?

By doing this, students generate new links within their own knowledge, allowing them to make rules which they can test. This is a process students can complete by themselves, but it is important to discuss these ideas beforehand, ensuring they have not picked up any incorrect ideas or misconceptions. Ideas such as elaborative interrogation (mentioned in the *Telling others what you know* section) and schematic representations (in Chapter 3) are useful ways of self-testing what you know using the three Cs.

How can we use self-testing using the three Cs?

An effective self-testing strategy is completing a 'brain dump'. Students are provided with a phrase or word crucial to the topic they are learning about. They are then asked to write down everything they know about this word or phrase. This allows for a quick examination of a student's schema, which has many benefits:

- Activates prior knowledge.

- Makes misconceptions transparent to the teacher, making them easier to tackle.
- Makes everyone engage with the content.
- Emphasises retrieval as a learning strategy.
- Allows students to generate links between areas of knowledge.

If we think carefully about how a brain dump is planned and sold to students, they can understand its effectiveness. It is important they understand how it works, and the conditions required to make it most effective:

- Complete the brain dump at the start of a lesson, or at a natural pausing point after an explanation.
- Provide a clearly defined topic that allows students to write everything they know about it.
- Ask students to close their books when they do this, as it should be information from their memory only.
- Either be specific with how you want them to write it (bullet points, mind map, on a whiteboard etc.) or give them a specific number of 'facts' to write.
- Review the task, being clear about how you can use this information going forward.

Once the brain dump is complete, it is important to use the information gathered to generate links between areas of knowledge that students know, which can be used to drive future learning. Brain dumps are high challenge, low threat activities, and their aim is to apply the three Cs to what students already know.

When trying to improve the quality of a brain dump so it can be used to apply the three Cs, it may be useful to use the following framework which encourages students to think in more detail about how their knowledge is structured, and therefore generate stronger links in their memory.

Specificity	Are the ideas specific to the subject or more general to 'common sense' knowledge of the topic?
Coherence	Do the points noted link together in a clear way, following the centrally decided theme?
Sequence	Are points noted down in an order that shows how ideas within a concept are linked?
Depth	Do the points go into a topic in detail, or do they just skim the surface of without discussing the core concepts?
Breadth	Is there a wide bank of knowledge about a topic that pushes the boundaries of other topics, or do the points only investigate one side of the topic?

Another useful way of generating knowledge and applying the three Cs is to use a Frayer model. This is a simple graphic organiser used for the development of concepts and vocabulary. It helps to guide students through a process of analysing the structure of a concept, which they can then use to compare, contrast and categorise with other concepts.

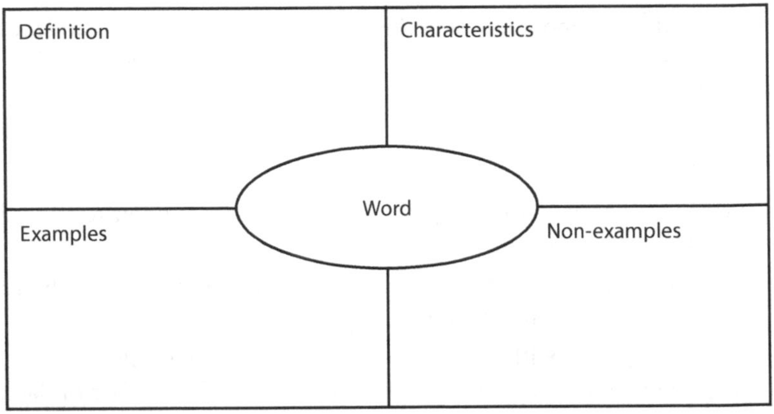
Definition
Characteristics
Word
Examples
Non-examples

The model allows students to see what a concept is and what it isn't, and so gain a further grasp of a topic. It does this by having four distinct sections; a definition, a set of characteristics, an example(s) of what the concept is, and a non-example(s) of what the concept isn't.

When using the Frayer model it is useful to go through the following steps:

- Describe the structure of the Frayer model to students before teaching a topic.
- Clearly define the key concepts or vocabulary you are going to teach.
- Signpost these key concepts and terms clearly to students.
- Model the process of using a Frayer model to the students and with the students.
- Show students how they can use the Frayer model independently to check they have fully understood a concept.
- Provide resources where students can check independently created Frayer models.
- Demonstrate how to use the Frayer model with the three Cs in relation to a variety of concepts, and therefore generate new learning.

Self-testing using the three Cs in action

- In **KS2** history by creating a brain dump to self-test a student's understanding of ancient Egypt and ancient Greece, and then **comparing** the two. This allows students to generate ideas around similar features of ancient civilizations.
- In **art** where students can be asked to **compare** and **contrast** artwork to help teach art history. For example, Renaissance versus Baroque, or Romanesque versus Gothic. This allows students to generate predictions about types of artwork in the history of art.
- In **business** where the Frayer model can be used to define and characterise different types of industries, allowing businesses to be **categorised**. For example, primary, secondary and tertiary industries. This allows students to generate ideas related to features of successful businesses in different sectors.

Why should we use spaced practice?

Shimamura discusses the idea of spaced retrieval practice in his book. He explains that re-reading textbooks and highlighting notes is ineffective, while self-generating information over a period of time can more than double the retention of key information.

> *The more often you self-generate material the better it will be established as a long-lasting memory. ... Students should space their retrieval practice across days. A rule of thumb is to divide your total study time into fifths and test yourself at each time point.*[48]

The science behind the technique of spaced retrieval practice, or spaced practice, is well known and has been discussed at great length, for example, by Pooja Agarwal in *How to use spaced retrieval practice to boost learning,*[49] and in Bjork's, *Memory and Meta-memory Considerations in the Training of Human Beings.*[50] The effectiveness of knowledge retention can be improved by reviewing material after an interval (spaced practice) rather than having a lengthy practice session in a single block (cramming, or massed or blocked practice). Spaced practice leads to better long-term results, while massed practice will only lead to short-term learning.

48. Shimamura, A. (2018), p32
49. Agarwal, P. & Carpenter, S. K. (2020). *How to use spaced retrieval practice to boost learning.* Retrieved from http://pdf.retrievalpractice.org/SpacingGuide.pdf
50. Bjork, R. (1994). Memory and meta-memory considerations in the training of human beings. In J. Metcalfe & A. Shimamura (Eds.) *Knowing about Knowing.* Cambridge, MA: MIT Press. Retrieved from https://bit.ly/3mlMOVQ

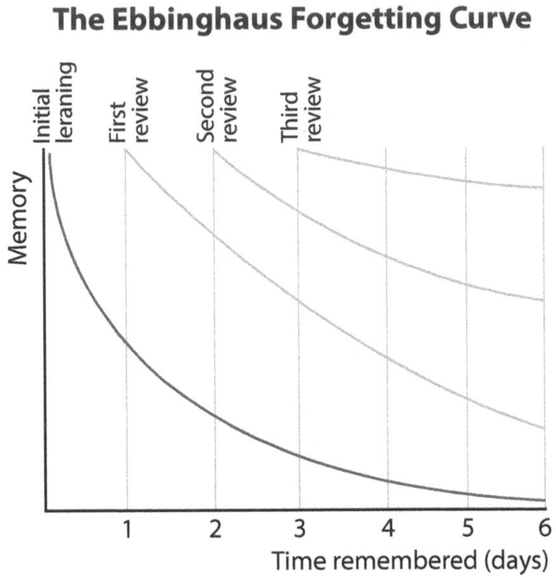
The Ebbinghaus Forgetting Curve
Initial leraning
First review
Second review
Third review
Memory
1
2
3
4
5
6
Time remembered (days)

While this intuitively makes sense to a teacher, students often do not see the benefit. They sometimes feel that their learning is slow and that they will have forgotten what they are learning now when they try to review it, or more often, that they will have forgotten what they are reviewing when they need to apply it in an assessment. A way to combat this is by demonstrating to students the power of spacing, and the importance of how it combats the Ebbinghaus forgetting curve.

The strength of knowledge deteriorates with time after it is first learned. If it is reviewed often, the strength of the knowledge increases again, and the rate at which the memory strength is lost reduces. This is the logic behind the common phrase, if you don't use it, you lose it. Through effective spaced practice, top-down processing is maximised, and students will be able to generate links between what they have just been taught and what they are reviewing, leading to a deeper understanding of the concepts involved.

How can we use spaced practice?

There are a series of key considerations to ensure spaced practice is effective:

- Model with students how to review work, not directly after it has been taught, but a few days after.

- Ensure students use effective self-learning strategies, for example self-testing, rather than just rereading notes.
- Suggest intervals of a few days or a week that students could build into their own review processes.
- Most importantly, direct students to review work related to topics they are studying so they can engage in top-down processing when generating links between knowledge.

Long gaps between intervals should lead to students needing to work harder to remember their prior learning, and therefore stronger links should be made. However, the intervals should not be so long that all of the prior learning has been forgotten.

The concepts of spacing should form an integral part of curriculum design. The way in which a subject is delivered should allow for students to reapply previously learned knowledge after an interval. However, this should not be an overriding factor as part of curriculum design; we should not be continually reviewing prior learning that has no relevance to what is about to be taught. Where it is not possible to build spaced practice into the flow of a curriculum, it could be built into a homework programme.

Spaced practice in action

- In **PE**, asking students to recall terms linked to a sport before teaching a related sport, for example rugby and football.
- In **science**, referring back to cells before teaching the respiratory system to allow students to generate links between the processes involved.
- In **computer science** when learning about aspects of software development, review work on the process of designing algorithms.

Case study: Business and economics at GCSE and A-level, Jade Pearce

All homework set for the classes I teach consists only of spaced retrieval practice; students are set retrieval practice activities to complete on topics they have learned previously.

A range of activities are used to ensure students do not get demotivated through using the same style of task. It also ensures that students practice retrieving their knowledge in different formats and that each topic is revisited multiple times.

When completing this independent work, students attempt each activity from memory before self-checking this using their notes to identify any errors or omissions. In the following lesson, we then discuss this as a class, allowing me to both check and cement learning. Finally, students use this spaced practice to identify those topics for which they need to complete further independent study.

For this homework to be completed effectively, it is crucial to teach students about memory and why strategies such as retrieval practice, spacing and interleaving are most effective for long-term learning. This makes it more likely that students would complete the tasks from memory, rather than using their notes which would seem easier but would not benefit their retention.

The embedding of spaced practice has resulted in students being able to recall much more of their knowledge than previously, and link areas of knowledge together. Students are also much more confident in their knowledge and this has increased their motivation and reduced their anxiety around any formal tests or examinations. Finally, the impact can be seen in outcomes – over the last two years 70-80% of pupils have achieved their best grade at both GCSE and A-Level with the Business and Economics department.

Jade Pearce leads on Teaching and Learning as an Assistant Headteacher at Walton High School in Stafford. She is also an Evidence Lead in Education at Staffordshire Research School. You can follow her and her work at @ PearceMrs.

Summary of Generate

In this chapter, we discussed the idea of a five-a-day challenge task to improve the retention of knowledge through elaborative interrogation, and the idea of telling others what you know. To improve the design of this task further, the idea of spacing could be built in. Within the example previously shown, the five ideas to be discussed linearly worked through the curriculum, day by day, to ensure complete curriculum coverage by a specific end point. This can be adapted to include the idea of spaced practice, by repeating relevant discussion points after a period of time. For example, Week two could include a review of topics from Week one to space out the process of elaborative interrogation, allowing students to generate links in their knowledge to aid the process of learning.

When summing up this chapter, I am reminded of a phrase I often say to students when encouraging them to engage in the process of practice: 'Contenders practice until they get it right, champions practice until they never get it wrong.' This helps to embed the idea that one of the ways to effectively generate new learning, is to practice talking about what you already know.

- Encourage students to engage in the process of elaboration by providing opportunities for them to tell others what they know.
- Use the generation effect and the production effect to allow students to apply what they have learned.
- Provide opportunities for self-testing, through elaborative interrogation and schematic organisation, using the three Cs.
- Use spaced practice as a tool to control the difficulty of review, and therefore affect the likelihood of retention of knowledge.

MARGE MODEL OF LEARNING: GENERATE: Reactivate learned information to enable memory consolidation			
	What it is ...	Focus on ...	Be wary of ...
Telling others what you know	Using ideas such as elaboration by encouraging students to talk through a topic, or write about it in detail.	Using specific topics for discussion to allow students an opportunity to showcase a wide depth of knowledge.	Being too open ended and not providing enough guidance within larger topics.
The generation effect and the production effect	Using cues and hints to encourage students to generate a response during encoding, and then doing something with the newly acquired knowledge.	Using these ideas during simple tasks that rely on applying knowledge pupils already know.	Playing 'guess what's in my head' by asking them to provide an answer when a topic has yet to be taught, or where the knowledge has not been retained.
Self-testing using the three Cs	Students practice applying and testing their own knowledge and make links between what they know by comparing, contrasting and categorising.	Reactivating what students already know and encouraging them to use the three Cs to generate new links between knowledge.	Making any form of self-testing too high stakes in accountability; the aim here is not to evaluate knowledge, but to draw links between it.
Spaced practice	Encouraging the review of material continually, over a period of time, rather than once close to the time of assessment, through the design of the curriculum and review materials.	Using spaced practice as an opportunity to link what students are reviewing to what they are learning. Reviewing content often enough to work against the Ebbinghaus forgetting curve.	Forgetting to create a culture of practice within the classroom. Leaving too long an interval between testing ideas where there are gaps in knowledge.

CHAPTER 5
E: EVALUATE

Chapter written by Jo Jukes

A student would not feel the need to study further if he/she felt that the material was already well learned.[51]

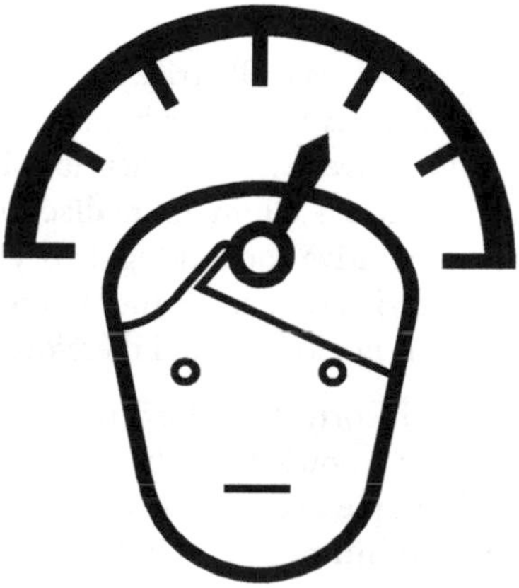

Shimamura says:[52]

Evaluate what you've learned:

- Delay evaluations to avoid the illusion of knowing.
- Test through generation.
- Construct your own key terms and test them using flashcards.
- Interleave topics by mixing up the order of testing.
- Test yourself, repeating to develop multiple paths to retrieval.

51. Shimamura, A. (2018), p34
52. Shimamura, A. (2018), p39

Within this chapter, these areas will be linked to the following strategies to encourage students to generate knowledge as part of long-term learning:

- Interleaving topics.
- Preventing the illusion of knowing.
- Flashcards.

Why do we need to evaluate our learning?

The fifth and final principle of the MARGE model is 'Evaluate'. Evaluation comes at the end of the learning cycle and requires students to metacognitively reflect on their learning. The question students need to consider is '*How do I know whether I have learned*?'

However, thinking metacognitively is really tricky, and needs to be taught. Often students overestimate their abilities and their knowledge, which leads them to incorrectly conclude that they have learned, when it is likely that they haven't. Throughout his chapter on 'Evaluate', Shimamura discusses a series of ideas that allow students to apply metacognitive and self-regulatory strategies which ensure they can effectively check that what they think they know, they actually do know, and also clearly identify what is not known and therefore needs to be relearned.

Occasionally, novice learners incorrectly believe themselves to be experts when given just a small amount of knowledge. This is a common effect, seen in many fields of research. A simple example is to consider statements made by people about public policy within politics. Quite often, after a small amount of research, people can feel confident about their knowledge of an area, and therefore overestimate their ability to communicate it. When asked questions around their understanding, often the presenter will realise the lack of depth in their understanding. Through developing their knowledge further, they can then develop their expertise, while being acutely aware of their limitations.

For our students, this can mean that once they understand the basics of a concept, they gain false confidence in their own abilities, believing themselves to be masters of the subject. This is problematic, as the false sense of understanding then becomes a barrier to effective evaluation.

Shimamura explains that there is '... a distinction between two kinds of metacognitive "knowing". There's hard-core knowing, which involves **recollection**, our ability to state explicitly why we know something ... and **familiarity**, that more diffuse "warmth" feeling of knowing that occurs when something is recognizable.'

> *I enter a friend's room and see on the wall a painting. At first I have the strange, wondering consciousness, 'surely I have seen that before,' but when or how does not become clear. There only clings to the picture a sort of penumbra of familiarity, – when suddenly I exclaim: 'I have it, it is a copy of part of one of the Fra Angelicos in the Florentine Academy – I recollect it there!'*
>
> *The Principles of Psychology.* William James. 1980

In the excerpt above[53] we can see both types of 'knowing' in action. The initial familiarity of '… I have seen that before' and thereafter, the recollection '… it is a copy of part of one of the Fra Angelicos in the Florentine Academy'.

So how do we get our students to evaluate their learning accurately? In essence, we need our students to understand the difference between the 'I recognise the painting' feeling of knowing and the concrete knowing of being able to say 'It's a Fra Angelico'. How do we get them to see that some knowledge does not make them an expert? Once they know the difference, they will be better placed to evaluate their own learning.

Throughout this chapter we will discuss ways in which students can evaluate their own learning, and the processes we can go through to ensure our evaluations are as accurate as they can be. While there is a theme of metacognition throughout, Shimamura also discusses specific key strategies that allow effective evaluation of learning:

1. **Interleaving topics** – mixing related topics while learning to test the robustness of what has been learned.
2. **Preventing the illusion of knowing** – engaging with processes to prevent over- or underestimations of what is known.
3. **Flashcards** – how they can be created and used to ensure knowledge has been retained over time and direct the next steps in learning.

Why should we interleave topics?

> *Interleaving occurs when different ideas or problem types are tackled in a sequence, as opposed to the more common method of attempting multiple versions of the same problem in a given study session.*[54]

53. Yonelinas, A., Wang, M., & Koen, J. (2010). Recollection and familiarity: examining controversial assumptions and new directions. *Hippocampus*, 20(11), 1178-1194. Retrieved from https://doi.org/10.1002/hipo.20864
54. Weinstein, Y., Madam, C., & Sumeracki, M. (2018). Teaching the science of learning. *Cognitive Research: Principles and Implications*, 3(2). Retrieved from https://bit.ly/3mu5Z00

When creating medium- and long-term schemes of learning, it is not unusual for us to cover one topic and then move onto the next, then the next, and so on. This approach is called 'blocking' or 'massing', and is traditionally how schools have approached delivery of content. However, if we interleave topics rather than mass or block them, then we are creating opportunities for topics to be revisited over time, which is much more effective for long-term learning.[55]

Massed Practice

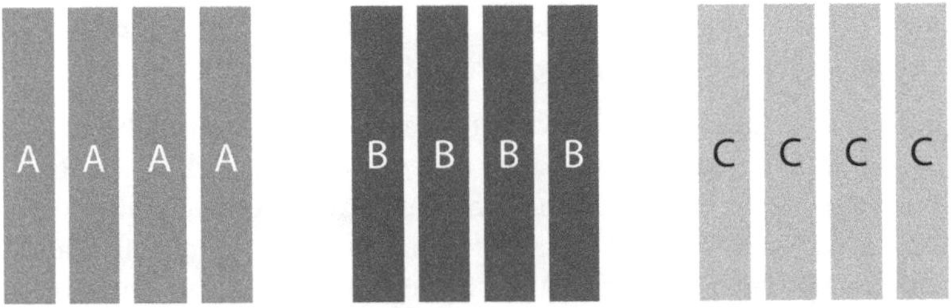
A A A A
B B B B
C C C C

Interleaved Practice

A C B C A C B A C B B A

The aim of interleaving is to create 'desirable difficulties'[56] where the process of recalling information through delivery and through testing is much more difficult for our students than if it was done in a more traditional 'blocked' (or massed) method.

Students are likely to feel more comfortable when delivery and testing is done using a blocked method, especially because they may falsely 'feel' that they are making more progress when studying one topic and then another, compared to interleaving, where they will naturally find the recall of content harder. Interleaving in testing

55. Czekala, B. (2020). *Interleaved practice – when and how to use it to maximize learning pace.* Retrieved from https://bit.ly/3cPBq1y
56. Bjork, R. (1994). Memory and meta-memory considerations in the training of human beings. In J. Metcalfe & A. Shimamura (Eds.) *Knowing about Knowing.* Cambridge, MA: MIT Press. Retrieved from https://bit.ly/3mlMOVQ

allows students to better evaluate their own knowledge, as by alternating topics, the strength of the understanding of topic areas can be more accurately evaluated. However, the long-term impacts of mixing topics either through delivery or through testing have been proven to be more beneficial to long-term learning. This is crucial when evaluating whether learning has taken place, as interleaving ensures that we are checking that links have been made in between topic areas.

How can we interleave topics?

In the classroom we can use it to plan delivery of content, so rather than delivering in a traditional blocked method we can revisit content in a structured and sequenced way. For example, in 'problem-based subjects, the interleaving technique is straightforward: simply mix questions on homework and quizzes with previous materials (which takes care of spacing as well); for languages, mix vocabulary themes rather than blocking by theme'.[57]

Interleaving can be used with spaced practice (a technique discussed in the *Generate* chapter), to ensure that we mix the content and delivery within topics as well as mixing related whole topics themselves together when learning and testing what has been learned. This is ideal for setting homework tasks that allow students to revisit previously covered material, and (particularly with older students) we can encourage them to use the technique in their own revision. By using interleaving in revision, especially when testing, students avoid only testing knowledge they have just reviewed, and therefore complete a more accurate evaluation of learning.

Interleaving topics in action

- In **economics**, set tasks where students have to complete supply and demand diagrams, income elasticity calculation questions, and price elasticity calculation questions in the same activity.
- In **science** when setting homework on motion, by also testing ideas such as forces, which link to why objects move.
- In **maths**, by asking students questions that link multiple areas of knowledge, such as volume, percentages, fractions and Pythagoras.

Why should we prevent the illusion of knowing?

The Dunning-Kruger effect is sometimes put forward as a way to explain why novices incorrectly believe themselves to be experts when given just a small amount

57. Thomson, R. & Mehring, J. (2016). Better vocabulary study strategies for long-term learning. *Kwansei Gakuin University Humanities Review*, 20, 133-141.

of knowledge. It is important to note that, although the validity of this effect is still up for debate,[58] it is not unusual for us to witness, as teachers, that our students can sometimes have false confidence in their own abilities, believing themselves to be masters of the subject when they have only a small amount of knowledge.

Psychologists refer to this concept as 'the illusion of knowing', when you think you know something because you are vaguely familiar with it. For our students, the 'illusion' of knowing taught content can be problematic because it stands in the way of the learning and evaluation process. Students can tell themselves 'I don't need to revise this, I already know it' when this is potentially not the case, they simply 'feel' like they know it.

It is often the case that students claim to understand some topics more than others. This is potentially because they are already familiar with some of the subject knowledge through past experiences and everyday life. The 'warm' familiarity of the content leads to a false sense of knowing.

A revision strategy I have seen many teachers use is RAG rating topics based on how well students 'feel' they already know them: 'If you know this well, highlight it in green, if you think it needs some revisiting, highlight it in orange, and if you don't know it very well, highlight it in red'. On the surface it appears to be a good starting point for revision as it aids students in highlighting priorities. However, the problem with this, when we acknowledge the concept of illusions of knowing, is that students are then less likely to revise topics they feel familiar with, despite the fact they may be unable to recall the specifics of them.

How can we prevent the illusion of knowing?

In *Make It Stick: The Science of Successful Learning*[59] several quizzing techniques are suggested to prevent illusions of knowing. In the previous chapter we discussed how the idea of self-testing against the three Cs can help with the generation of links between areas of knowledge; these techniques can also be used to evaluate students' learning, to check that they have learned what they should have learned and are ready to move on.

One of the most effective methods of self-quizzing I have seen in use is the knowledge quiz; a simple set of questions with the answers provided. Students are then tested on the answers to these questions over a period of weeks to ensure they have not only learned this core knowledge, but also have retained

58. Jarry, J. (2020, December 27). *The Dunning-Kruger effect is probably not real.* Retrieved from https://bit.ly/3dAwf4z
59. Brown, P., McDaniel, M., & Roediger, H. (2014). *Make it Stick: The Science of Successful Learning.* Cambridge, MA: Harvard University Press.

it to generate links to future learning. Ways in which these knowledge quizzes can be used include:

- pre-topic, to check what knowledge is already known, and to inform future instruction
- during a topic, to check on the effectiveness of instruction, and allow what has been taught to be built on further
- post-topic, to check for coverage on content and that the key knowledge required for a topic has been understood.

Thinking back to the *Motivate* chapter of this book, providing students with the big picture of a topic can be motivating as it allows them to see what they are aiming for. This lends itself to a process of not only providing the questions, but the answers that go with them too.

A process for implementing knowledge quizzes with students could be:

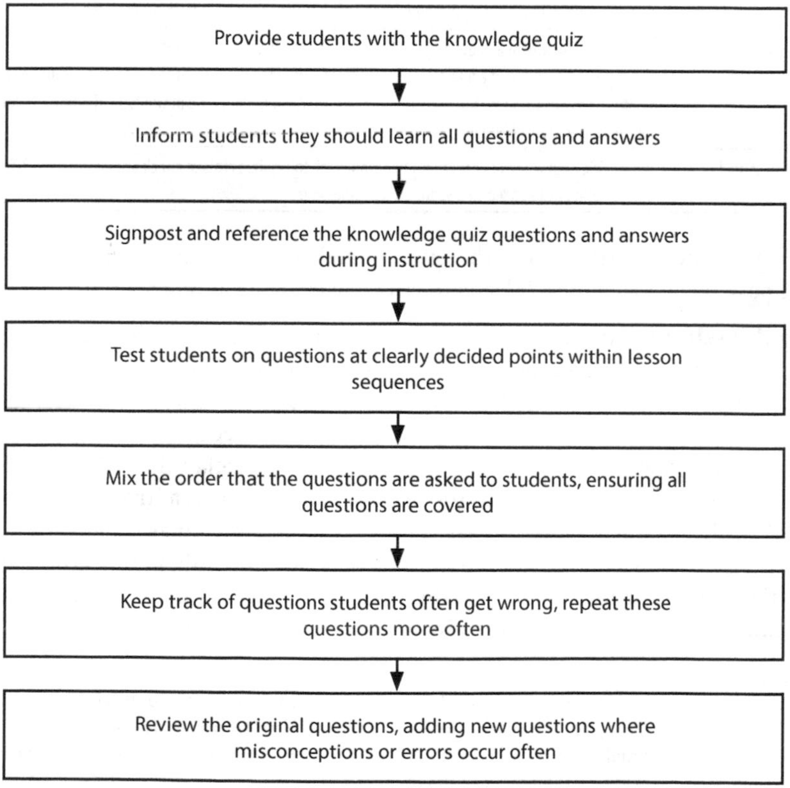
Provide students with the knowledge quiz
Inform students they should learn all questions and answers
Signpost and reference the knowledge quiz questions and answers during instruction
Test students on questions at clearly decided points within lesson sequences
Mix the order that the questions are asked to students, ensuring all questions are covered
Keep track of questions students often get wrong, repeat these questions more often
Review the original questions, adding new questions where misconceptions or errors occur often

Self-quizzing materials have huge potential to build students' confidence in being able to review their learning in readiness for applying it, be that in examinations or in a lesson where it needs to be applied to new concepts. This allows effective evaluation of the knowledge so students know whether they are ready to move on. It is crucial, therefore, that when constructing materials that are to be used for self-quizzing, care is taken to ensure that they can be used by students independently, and they contain the right knowledge to prepare students for their next steps. Some considerations when creating a knowledge quiz include:

Content selection	Select the content that will have the most impact on student understanding within the subject; these concepts are often known as threshold concepts, or threshold knowledge.
Breadth versus depth	Decide whether the quiz should cover a large domain of the topic in little detail, or focus on a small domain in significant detail.
Number of questions	Most knowledge quizzes contain between 10 to 20 questions. The number of questions relies on the amount of content that needs to be covered, and the breadth and depth required.
Specificity of answers	Answers should be specific and should allow students to learn them alongside the question to develop their understanding of a topic. They should also allow self-marking to take place.
Cognitive demand	While the structure of a knowledge quiz focuses on recall questions, context can be used to vary the cognitive demand of a question. For example, 'What is the name of the type of bonding that happens between metals and non-metals?' versus 'What is the name of the type of bonding that happens in sodium chloride?'
Clarity of goal	Be specific with what you are trying to obtain with this quiz. Is this to check prior knowledge? To assess what has been learned within a recent lesson?

Alongside the construction of the quiz, it is also important to consider how it will be delivered to ensure it leads to effective evaluation of learning.

Regular self-quizzing involves students writing down what they know about a concept by answering a series of questions, and then checking whether their knowledge is accurate, needs correcting or requires further development, allowing students to evaluate their strength of knowledge. In *Battle Hymn of the Tiger Teachers,*[60] Joe Kirby talks about how, at Michaela School, homework *is* self-quizzing; in fact, he refers to the homework strategy as a 'five-year revision plan'[61] which also deals with the issue of revision being seen as something done at the end of a key stage, in preparation for an exam. This allows students to clearly identify for themselves whether they know something or need to review it again. 'One of the best habits to instil in a learner is regular self-quizzing.'[62]

60. Birbalsingh, K. (2016). *Battle Hymn of the Tiger Teachers.* Woodbridge: John Catt.
61. Kirby, J. (2015, May 3). *A 5-year revision plan.* Retrieved from https://bit.ly/3uq8Zgq
62. Brown, P., McDaniel, M., & Roediger, H. (2014). *Make it stick: the science of successful learning.* Cambridge, MA: Harvard University Press.

Frequent low-stakes quizzes test students' knowledge but have no impact on their overall grade. Ensuring that content is covered from across the course, rather than the content most recently covered, is an important part of the process. Low-stakes quizzes can be integrated into lessons, for example, as a starter task as shown below. In this example, content is quizzed from this week, last week, last month and last term, which is deliberately planned to reflect what we know about the importance of spacing, forgetting and retrieval. Low-stakes quizzes are useful for us as teachers as they allow us to see potential gaps in knowledge and areas we may need to revisit, but they are equally useful for students in preventing illusions of knowing as they can very quickly see whether they are able to recall knowledge accurately across the range of content.

This week 1. Draw a fully labelled supply and demand diagram.	Last week 2. Give two factors that influence demand and two factors that influence supply.
Last month 3. How is market growth calculated?	Last term 4. Give one benefit and one drawback of setting up as a private limited company.

Cumulative quizzing may come at the end of a unit of work or at a specified time – such as end of year assessments – and cover content from across the whole course rather than the most recently covered material. Cumulative quizzes that cover a range of previously covered material are the most effective as they enable students to not only revisit recent content, but to make connections with new content. Research carried out in 2013 found that students who studied for cumulative tests were more likely to retain knowledge than those who were tested at the end of a module of work.[63] This is useful, as too often in 'end of unit' tests that cover only the most recent material, we are not checking the depth of a students' knowledge or evaluating whether it has been retained over time. A better way to assess

63. Khanna, M., Badura-Brack, A., & Finken, L. (2013). Short- and long-term effects of cumulative finals on student learning. *Teaching of Psychology*, 40(3), 175-182. Retrieved from https://doi.org/10.1177/0098628313487458

students would be to build previously covered material into the tests, so that over time, the 'end of unit' tests become a cumulative assessment of the whole course.

Preventing the illusion of knowing in action

- In **history**, at the end of a unit on the French Revolution, create a cumulative assessment that includes questions about the Normans and The Black Death.
- In **KS2 English** with spellings, start each lesson with a test that covers suffixes, prefixes, compound words, etymology and letter strings, and then link this to a RAG rating sheet that evaluates learning more accurately.
- In **geography**, where we can test knowledge using carefully designed multiple choice questions to check whether key knowledge of coastal processes is understood, as this knowledge will be built on in KS4 when teaching longshore drift.

Case study: English at KS3 and KS4, Rebecca Lee

We provide all students in KS3 and KS4 with a knowledge organiser for the text they are studying. These set out the key information we want every student to know. The information on the knowledge organiser is that which we want all students to be able to recall with ease, which will free up working memory when they are tackling challenging skills such as writing an essay on a text.

We have given every student an exercise book which is just for their self-quizzing homework and we expect every student from Year 7 up to Year 11 to spend a minimum of 30 minutes every week self-quizzing on their knowledge organiser. We would expect to look in their self-quizzing book and see a minimum of a page of evidence of them self-quizzing every week. This is something as a teacher I can check in a few minutes at the start or end of a lesson by asking students to open their self-quizzing books and quickly walking around the room to check if it has been done. Students' progress is visible to them as they flick through their books and see what they could recall at the start and what they can now recall.

In terms of the impact, positive effects in terms of both knowledge retention and students' confidence can be witnessed.

> Our pupils really know their stuff – we know they're learning and retaining the information on the knowledge organisers we've given them because most lessons begin with a five-a-day retrieval practice starter and we're seeing more and more students achieving five out of five. Students' confidence is improving too because they can see how much more they now know.[64]
>
> *Rebecca Lee is an Assistant Headteacher, in charge of Teaching and Learning at Wyvern St Edmunds School in Salisbury. She tweets at @TLPMrsL*

Why should we use flashcards?

Shimamura explains that much of learning is about making connections between concepts. This 'often depends on remembering cued or pairwise associations, such as new terms, definitions, or foreign vocabulary words'[65] so he suggests creating a set of key terms and then self-testing using flashcards.

Flashcards encourage retrieval and drill, and if used effectively allow for spacing and overcoming forgetting. We can also encourage metacognitive skills if we guide students to make their own flashcards and use them to monitor their own learning. So many teachers love flashcards because they pull together so many of the skills that we know are important in developing effective, long-term learning.

How can we use flashcards?

Flashcards are a method of revision and study that are used by many students, but they must be created and used effectively to have the most impact. Research carried out in 2012 shows that students often cheat when using flashcards, either by turning them over too quickly instead of thinking hard about the answer, or by falsely assuming they already know the content and removing them from their pack of cards.[66]

In her 2019 blog[67] cognitive scientist Pooja Agarwal outlines three methods to make the use of flashcards effective:

64. Lee, R. (2018, January 13). *On self-quizzing homework*. Retrieved from https://bit.ly/3cNTMQp
65. Shimamura, A. (2018), p39
66. Wissman, K., Rawson, K., & Pyc, M. (2012). How and when do students use flashcards? *Memory*, 20(6), 568-579. Retrieved from https://doi.org/10.1080/09658211.2012.687052
67. Agarwal, P. (2020). *Make flashcards more powerful with these 3 tips*. Retrieved from https://bit.ly/2PZ6WRw

Retrieve	The aim of using a flashcard is to ensure students retrieve the answer to a question, either by writing it down or saying it out loud. This overcomes the idea of the illusion of knowing by ensuring students can self-check the answers to make accurate evaluations about what they know.
Re-order	Shuffle the deck of flashcards before each attempt at using them. This increases the level of challenge by adding the concepts of interleaving and spacing to the ideas being tested.
Repeat	Repeatedly check learning by using the same flashcard. Just because a card has been correctly answered once, it doesn't mean it shouldn't be checked again. Leave a flashcard in a deck until the answer has been correctly retrieved three times.

It is important therefore, to explicitly model effective use of flashcards to students. An example of an effective method of incorporating flashcards into schemes of learning could be by providing students with a stack of cards and at the end of each lesson, or series of lessons, asking students to write their flashcards using the key terms and concepts that have been covered in those lessons. These cards can then be integrated into lesson starters or activities.

Another strategy is where students put their flashcards into three RAG boxes; a red box for 'I don't feel confident that I know about this topic'; amber for 'I feel I know this topic quite well', and green for 'I feel confident I know this topic.' The problem with this is that it encourages illusions of knowing, so should only be used in conjunction with the 'Retrieve, Re-order, Repeat' methods above.

A simple strategy for modelling the idea of how often a flashcard should be used is the Leitner system:

> *The Leitner system developed by Sebastian Leitner in 1972 is a simple design to enhance memory retention. In the Leitner system, flashcards are grouped into packs of increased levels of memory retention – or current levels of knowledge. Correct answers progress a flashcard to a higher-level pack, incorrect answers revert a flashcard to the lowest level pack. Common Leitner systems have five levels of flashcard packs.*[68]

The key to using this system is twofold:

- Lower-level flashcard decks are reviewed more often, for example daily, while higher-level decks are reviewed less frequently, such as weekly or monthly.
- As flashcards are repeatedly answered correctly they move up towards the higher level decks, while if cards are answered incorrectly, they move towards the lower decks.

---

68. Colbran, S. (2018). *Flashcards and spaced repetition fending off forgetfulness.* Ascilite 2018. Retrieved from 10.13140/RG.2.2.16611.40485

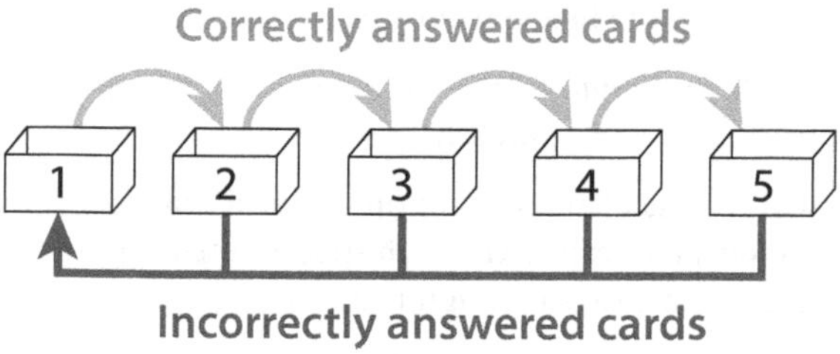
Correctly answered cards
1
2
3
4
5
Incorrectly answered cards

This helps students evaluate their own learning, as at a glance they will be able to tell which concepts or questions they understand better than others; the higher the deck a question is in, the better that knowledge has been retained.

Flashcards in action

- In **PE** within the area of anatomy and physiology, to better understand which systems within the body are known and can be retrieved, and which need reviewing again.
- In **music**, put pictures of instruments on one side of the card, and the name of the instrument and the instrument family on the other side. Students can put the flashcards picture side up and test if they know the name of the instrument and the family it belongs to.
- In **KS1** flashcards can be used to help teach phonics, with the sound on one side of the card and the phrase on the other, or to help remember common expectation words, with the word on one side of the card, and the word within a sentence on the other side.

Summary of Evaluate

Evaluating learning can be a difficult concept; it is so much more than providing students with a test. We need to provide students with resources that allow them to overcome the illusion of knowing and accurately check whether they are capable of retaining and retrieving knowledge over a period of time. Guiding students through the process of self-evaluation and reflection on their performance allows them to clearly define the next steps in their learning, fill knowledge gaps and prepare themselves for what comes next.

When summarising this chapter, it is vital to recognise the importance both to students and staff of accurately assessing and understanding students' knowledge levels, and achieving this by using a variety of evaluative strategies.

This is not a new idea, indeed, is it one that was not lost on philosophers in the past. As shown in the quote below from Epictetus, a Greek stoic philosopher:

For it is impossible for a man to begin to learn what he has a conceit that he already knows.[69]

The strategies within this chapter build on the idea that accurate evaluation of learning relies on repeated testing through spaced retrieval practice, and testing via multiple retrieval pathways through interleaving.

Modelling the use of metacognition and self-regulation within the classroom helps students use it to evaluate their own processes of learning. The strength of this evaluation can be improved by:

- Strategically interleaving topics to increase the difficulty of retrieving knowledge for students, to ensure that when they are evaluating what they have learned it is embedded.
- Encouraging students to consider the illusion of knowing and consider whether they are just familiar with a topic rather than know it and can apply that knowledge.
- Using flashcards effectively to check what is known and create a process to check what needs to be learned next.

69. Epictetus (2009). *The Golden Sayings of Epictetus* (H. Crossley, Trans.). EZreads Publications.

MARGE MODEL OF LEARNING: EVALUATE: How do we know what we know?			
	What it is ...	Focus on ...	Be wary of ...
Interleaving topics	Switching between topics and ideas during the learning or review process. The opposite of massed or blocked practice.	Interleaving related topics. Using interleaving to add desirable difficulty and make learning 'harder' to test the strength of retention and retrieval of knowledge.	Massed or blocked practice, where only one area of knowledge is assessed at one time. Interleaving topics that are unrelated leading to confusion.
The illusion of knowing	The idea that students feel they have understood a concept and have a good grasp of it, when their understanding is only at a surface level.	Using self-testing as a diagnostic tool that allows students to evaluate the relocation of their knowledge, and find areas of strength and areas for improvement. Creating low-stakes quizzes and activities that allow students to work independently of the teacher.	Using RAG activities that are based on students' familiarity with an area of knowing, rather than evaluating how well it has been recalled. Creating evaluation tasks where the answers are too vague for the students to use independently of the teacher.
Flashcards	Creating cards where on one side there is a key term or an idea, and on the other there is an explanation of a concept; this is used to check that key concepts have been understood and retained.	Using the retrieve, re-order and repeat method. Mixing related topics through effective interleaving and flashcard use. Using the Leitner system to evaluate whether knowledge has been learned and can be recalled.	Imprecise terminology being used on the flashcards, that can lead to misconceptions building. Too much content on the answer side of the card. Students discarding cards, or reviewing them less often, after only correctly recalling them once.

CHAPTER 6
A WHOLE-BRAIN MODEL OF LEARNING

With MARGE in hand, you now have tools for efficient learning. The five principles should be applied at all stages of learning – during class sessions, reading textbook material, and studying for exams.[70]

MARGE has refined the way I think about the learning process. It provides a clear framework that encompasses many of the key factors that affect learning not only within the classroom, but also outside it.

MARGE should be considered as an acronym used as a narrative through the learning process. Students need to be **motivated** to learn the topic at hand. Their **attention** should be focussed on the core knowledge and skills required from the activity at hand. Students should be **relating** this knowledge to what they already know, and begin the process of **generating** links between areas of knowledge. Through repeated **relate-generate-evaluate** cycles students can then assess the robustness of their understanding of topics, and ensure that what they have learned is stored in long-term memory. When students are not learning effectively, MARGE forms a useful framework for discussion around what could potentially be improved.

It is important to not just treat MARGE as a checklist. We cannot look at a lesson and think, this lesson needs more M or this lesson needs more G. Each of the elements within MARGE cannot be addressed in isolation because they are intrinsically linked. A criticism of this book could be that it has treated each of the elements of MARGE in isolation in five separate chapters. However, each chapter has offered potential ideas to engage with the MARGE model of learning, and these ideas could be built on further using the entire model. For example, when discussing self-testing in the *Evaluate* chapter, if they were given to students before a topic, quizzes could be used to motivate students by providing them with the big picture, and could also focus their attention by making the learning goals clear.

As Shimamura says on multiple occasions, learning is a whole-brain issue:

70. Shimamura, A. (2018), p42

When we acknowledge the fact that learning is a whole-brain issue, we can develop a more comprehensive approach to brain-based learning programs.[71]

This confirms the point that all aspects of MARGE need to be considered when discussing learning. It is important to ask questions about how what we are doing within the classroom can be improved by the framework of MARGE, rather than considering what aspects of MARGE are missing.

The table below highlights a series of questions that could be used to guide a conversation about the ideas included in MARGE.

Motivate	Do students: • Grasp the narrative of repeating themes within a subject? • Understand why they are being taught what they are being taught, and how it links to the world around them? • Show curiosity in what is being taught? • Have opportunities to share their thoughts on what they are learning?
Attend	Are students aware of: • What they need to focus their attention on in each lesson? • How what they are learning links to what they already know? • How what they are learning forms part of a bigger process of what they are learning within the subject?
Relate	Are students guided to: • Use a variety of strategies to relate what they are being taught to what they already know? • Learn using a variety of sources including visual imagery and schematic representations? • Compare, contrast and categorise what they know with what they are being taught?
Generate	Do students have opportunities to: • Share what they have learned with their peers and at home? • Use what they already know to form new ideas? • Apply what they have just learned in a different context? • Link knowledge through self-testing using the three Cs? ? • Revisit learning after a period of time to check they have remembered it?
Evaluate	Are students aware of how to: • Interleave topics and use spaced practice to evaluate the strength of concepts in their long-term memory? • Avoid potential pitfalls, such as the illusion of knowing? • Construct flashcards and other tools to effectively test the strength of learning?

71. Shimamura, A. (2018, July 21). *The power and pitfalls of brain-based learning programs.* Retrieved from https://bit.ly/3mmOE9g

Through discussing the process of learning using these questions, teachers can begin to think about how they can adapt their practice to make it more effective. This isn't about doing something new, or different; it is about refining what we are doing to ensure we maximise the impact it has.

It is important to remember here that when we discuss whole-brain learning processes, we are not discussing the ideas of learning styles, or how different parts of the brain lend themselves to different ways of learning.

> *Although there may be subtle differences in the way individuals process information, there is no evidence to suggest that educational practices should be geared differently for so-called different learning styles. MARGE will benefit all students by fostering broad-based active learning skills.*[72]

Shimamura makes it clear that MARGE, as a whole-brain learning strategy, will benefit all learners. Much of what he discusses is evident in primary and secondary classrooms, as exemplified by the case studies and practical suggestions mentioned throughout this book. As a model of learning MARGE allows educators to consider a wide variety of ideas from cognitive science. Key to the concept of MARGE is the idea of top-down processing; learning is not soaked up, instead we use what we know to direct and select relevant information that can be added to our existing schema.

MARGE is a clear model for learning, rooted in neuroscience and cognitive science, and understanding it allows us to consider how it can be used as a whole to refine the tools we use to help students review learning.

MARGE and knowledge organisers

Knowledge organisers are an aid to support learning; it is how they are used that makes them part of a learning strategy. Too often the thought process behind what is required to make a learning strategy more effective has not been thoroughly thought through. MARGE can help with this by providing a framework for the implementation of learning aids.

> *Given the principles presented here, educators have the tools to foster more efficient student learning. Simple aids during class include 1) displaying on screen or providing handouts of main points (schema) in outline form, 2) spending several minutes at the beginning of class engaging motivation with the big picture using key questions, real-world analogies, demonstrations, or personal anecdotes, and 3) encouraging retrieval practice with question/answer periods.*[73]

72. Shimamura, A. (2018), p43
73. Shimamura, A. (2018), p43

A well constructed knowledge organiser will fulfill the criteria shared by Shimamura. It will provide students with an outline of the key points within a topic, providing the big picture. By linking the knowledge to be covered to the real world, students may be more motivated to cover the topic as they can see contextual links. Key points and threshold concepts can also be highlighted effectively within a knowledge organiser; when staff are talking through the knowledge organiser they can signpost these, ensuring students know exactly what they need to attend to. Knowledge organisers can also be used to effectively show the links between areas of knowledge, especially through schematic representations. If they are then coupled with a set of questions from a knowledge quiz or a simple self-testing activity, students can engage with the process of generating new learning and evaluating the effectiveness of their learning.

MARGE can therefore be used to help guide the thoughts and considerations that need to be taken into account when creating and using a knowledge organiser.

Does the knowledge organiser:

- show enough of the big picture?
- highlight key areas of knowledge that students must pay close attention to?

Can the knowledge organiser be used to:

- show links between areas of knowledge?
- allow students to engage in self-testing using the three Cs, generating new learning?
- ensure students can evaluate the effectiveness of their knowledge of the topic?

Alongside these questions, we should also consider the suitability of a knowledge organiser. For example, when I was discussing the use of knowledge organisers with a primary colleague, she lamented the fact that more often than not the contents are not matched to the reading age of the pupils. If this is the case, it would be difficult for students to use it for self-testing and to evaluate the effectiveness of their knowledge. It would also lead to students feeling unmotivated about the topic, as they would feel too much of the content is inaccessible.

After using knowledge organisers throughout her time preparing for her GCSE examinations, a student approached me with one that she had created at the end of her A-level physics course, which can be seen on the next page. It was interesting to see how she put it together and whether the principles I had used to design my own were present in my students' work. While many aspects were present (a clear design, related concepts close to each other to show links, key ideas boxed off and underlined), ideas relating to generating new learning through using the three Cs and evaluating the learning process were missing. As I was having this discussion with the student just after reading MARGE, I talked through the learning process with her, and we discussed how she could improve her resource.

The next day she returned with a table of questions on the back of the knowledge organiser. Next to each question was a simple system of organising which questions needed reviewing more or less often than others.

Through a simple process, the use of a learning aid became more effective and aligned with key ideas from the learning sciences. While this is in no way a magic bullet that fixes all the problems with knowledge organisers (Sam Hall has written an excellent blog on this topic, *Knowledge Organisers – A Failed Revolution*[74]) it allows their use to become more refined and have greater impact.

74. Hall, S. (2020, July 25). *Knowledge organisers – a failed revolution.* Retrieved from https://bit.ly/3mkQS8S

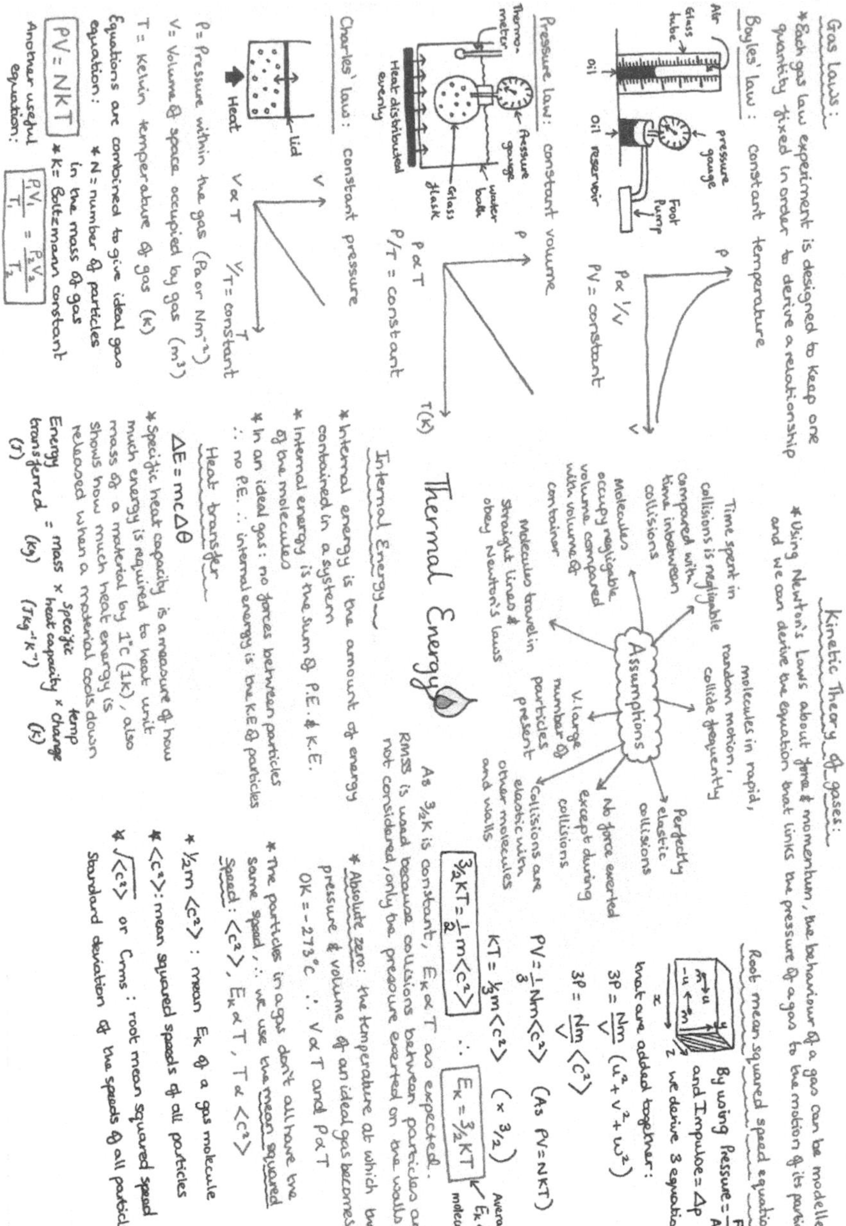
Gas Laws:
* Each gas law experiment is designed to keep one quantity fixed in order to derive a relationship
Boyles' law: constant temperature
Air
Glass tube
pressure gauge
Foot Pump
Oil
Oil reservoir
P
V
P ∝ 1/V
PV = constant
Pressure law: constant volume
Thermo-meter
Pressure gauge
water bath
Glass flask
Heat distributed evenly
P
T(K)
P ∝ T
P/T = constant
Charles' law: constant pressure
lid
Heat
V
T
V ∝ T
V/T = constant
P = Pressure within the gas (Pa or Nm⁻²)
V = Volume of space occupied by gas (m³)
T = Kelvin temperature of gas (K)
Equations are combined to give ideal gas equation:
PV = NKT
* N = number of particles in the mass of gas
* K = Boltzmann constant
Another useful equation:
P₁V₁/T₁ = P₂V₂/T₂
Kinetic Theory of gases:
* Using Newton's Laws about force & momentum, the behaviour of a gas can be modelled and we can derive the equation that links the pressure of a gas to the motion of its particles
Assumptions
Time spent in collisions is negligable compared with time inbetween collisions
molecules in rapid, random motion, collide frequently
Perfectly elastic collisions
No force exerted except during collisions
Collisions are elastic with other molecules and walls
V. large number of particles present
Molecules travel in straight lines & obey Newton's laws
Molecules occupy negligable volume compared with volume of container
Root mean squared speed equation
By using Pressure = F/A and Impulse = Δp we derive 3 equations that are added together:
3P = Nm/V (u² + v² + w²)
3P = Nm/V ⟨c²⟩
PV = 1/3 Nm⟨c²⟩ (As PV = NKT)
KT = 1/3 m⟨c²⟩ (× 3/2)
3/2 KT = 1/2 m⟨c²⟩
∴ E_K = 3/2 KT
Average E_K of molecules
As 3/2 K is constant, E_K ∝ T as expected.
RMSS is used because collisions between particles are not considered, only the pressure exerted on the walls.
Thermal Energy
Internal Energy
* Internal energy is the amount of energy contained in a system
* Internal energy is the sum of P.E. & K.E. of the molecules
* In an ideal gas: no forces between particles ∴ no P.E. ∴ internal energy is the K.E of particles
Heat transfer
ΔE = mcΔθ
* Specific heat capacity is a measure of how much energy is required to heat unit mass of a material by 1°C (1K), also shows how much heat energy is released when a material cools down
Energy transferred (J) = mass (kg) × specific heat capacity (JKg⁻¹K⁻¹) × temp change (K)
* Absolute zero: the temperature at which the pressure & volume of an ideal gas becomes 0.
0K = -273°C ∴ V ∝ T and P ∝ T
* The particles in a gas don't all have the same speed, ∴ we use the mean squared speed: ⟨c²⟩, E_K ∝ T, T ∝ ⟨c²⟩
* 1/2 m ⟨c²⟩ : mean E_K of a gas molecule
* ⟨c²⟩: mean squared speeds of all particles
* √⟨c²⟩ or Crms : root mean squared speed
Standard deviation of the speeds of all particles

A-Level physics knowledge organiser created by a student

MARGE and SQ3R

In his book, Shimamura also discusses the link between MARGE and other popular study tools, including the SQ3R method,[75] a technique used when reading to help students absorb information. SQ3R stands for Survey, Question, Read, Recite and Review.

S: Survey	Survey or skim the text, taking note of the main headings and features, and summary paragraphs. This should only take three to five minutes.
Q: Question	Generate questions about what has been read: What is the text about? What am I trying to learn by reading this text?
R: Read	Using information from S and Q, engage in active reading, allowing the questions generated in Q to be answered.
R: Recite	From memory, recite the information that has been learned through reading and answering the questions from Q.
R: Review	At the end of each section, review the text, repeating back the key points from each section in your own words. This entire process then repeats.

The link between SQ3R and MARGE is clearly explained by Shimamura. Surveying the text allows students to access the big picture, which within MARGE has links to **motivation**. Questions being created about the text allow the engagement of top-down processing, focussing **attention** on key chunks of information. When reading the text, information should be **related** to existing knowledge, building meaning. Reciting information allows the **generation** of links between knowledge and the movement of it to long-term memory through the process of elaboration and practice. Reviewing what has been learned allows the **evaluation** of learning to take place, through effective metacognitive strategies.

MARGE and Cornell note taking

Cornell note taking is another useful study tool which can be used to create notes that facilitate effective revision. While there are many templates that exist, they all follow a similar format:

- The page or paper is divided up into key sections.
- These sections include a focus on:
    - the overarching topic
    - key questions
    - brief notes
    - a summary of the page.

75. Shimamura, A. (2018), p44

- Changes in topic should be signified through effective use of bullet point notes.

While there is no prescribed way to use Cornell note taking,[76] its effective use as a study tool generally relies on the following:

- A complete, legible, and accurate set of notes.
- The summary should be completed once the notes section is completed, sometimes after a period of delay.
- The key questions should be used to test understanding, either through elaboration or retrieval practice.

Physics teacher and blogger Gethyn Jones has written an excellent post on how ideas from the Ebbinghaus forgetting curve can be implemented into Cornell note taking.[77] Jones' blog contains a process that begins with students completing their notes based around the main question. They then wait 24 hours before completing the key questions and key words section. After a further 48 hours, students then write a summary of what they have learned. By building in this idea of review after an interval, spaced practice has become part of the process. As discussed in Chapter 4 *G: Generate*, spaced practice is an effective technique to encourage students to engage with generating links between areas of knowledge.

The MARGE model of learning can be explicitly linked to areas of the Cornell notes template. The 'big question' **motivates** students by providing them with the big picture. The key words and key questions focus students on what areas of knowledge they need to **attend** to. The notes section allows students to **relate** knowledge and **generate** learning through applying the three Cs when note taking and elaborating on key points, as well as using diagrams to aid explanations. The summary section allows students to **evaluate** their learning and look at how spaced practice can be used to assess the robustness of their knowledge. Students could also use the summary section, along with the key words and key questions to construct flashcards that can be used to assess their learning.

76. Cornell University (Retrieved 2020). *Cornell note-taking: note-taking strategies*. Cornell University. https://bit.ly/3wrorLc
77. Jones, G. (2020, August 26). *Cornell versus Ebbinghaus*. Retrieved from https://bit.ly/3sSolKr

<table>
<tr>
<td>Key questions and key words:</td>
<td>Big question:

What processes take place in rivers and how do they change throughout a river?</td>
</tr>
<tr>
<td>1. What is erosion?

2. How does transportation occur?

3. What is deposition?

4. How can we use river profiles?

Erosion
Transportation
Deposition
River profiles
Upper course
Lower course
Mouth
Source</td>
<td>Notes:

Load - the particles carried by the water
Source - where the river starts
Mouth - where river meets the sea
Upper course - near where the river starts - large load
Lower course - near flatter land - load is fine sediment

1. Erosion
a. Abrasion - pebbles grind along river bank and bed
b. Attrition - rocks carried by water hit against each other creating smaller rounder rocks
c. Hydraulic action - water smashes into banks, trapping air in cracks causing rocks to break off
d. Solution - rocks dissolve within water e.g. limestone

2. Transportation
a. Traction - pebbles rolled along river bed (near source)
b. Saltation - pebbles bounced along river bed (near source)
c. Suspension - lightsediment carried within water (near mouth)
d. Solution - dissolved chemicals moved within water

3. Deposition
a. Dropping material when the river loses energy
b. Caused by:
i. Shallower water
ii. Volume of water has decreased
iii. At the river's mouth

4. River profiles
a. Long profile
i. A line from source to the mouth
ii. Shows river changes over its course
b. Cross profile
i. A cross-section of the river</td>
</tr>
<tr>
<td colspan="2">Review:
The key processes within a river are erosion, transportation and deposition. We can examine river profiles to see how they change throughout a river's course. Different forms of erosion and transportation occur at different parts within a river as the energy of the river and depth of water vary.</td>
</tr>
</table>

Example of completed Cornell notes on the topic of river processes

MARGE and the Feynman technique

The Feynman technique is a mental model used to convey information using concise thoughts and simple language. The technique is a four-stage process:

- Identify a subject.
- Teach it to a child.
- Identify and fill your knowledge gaps.
- Organise, simplify and tell your story.

When identifying a subject you should write down, in a concise way, everything you know about it. Take these notes, and then work with them so you can teach the topic to a child, elaborating on ideas using simple language and diagrams. The language used should be accessible to all, and the communication should be precise. Highlighting knowledge gaps in your explanations ensures that you stitch your schema together and fill these gaps with missing knowledge. Once this is complete, you can then explain a topic in detail, in simple language, precisely and with a narrative. This needs clear organisation of your thoughts and explanations.

Feynman argued that if all scientific knowledge were destroyed, the following sentence would allow future society to rebuild the current body of knowledge that exists in science:

> *All things are made of atoms – little particles that move around in perpetual motion, attracting each other when they are a little distance apart, but repelling upon being squeezed into one another.*[78]

This sentence exemplifies the Feynman technique. By being precise, having a clear narrative, and using language free of jargon, it makes it clear what to attend to, and motivates the reader to want to know more about the topic. The Feynman technique acts not only as a useful study tool for the creator of the sentence, but also as a tool to guide future learning for the recipient.

The MARGE model of learning has many parallels to the Feynman technique:

- **Motivation** can be piqued by delivering an explanation as a story.
- The process of identifying the subject focusses the **attention** of the person crafting the explanation, as well as the learner.
- Through teaching it using simple language, **relational links** are **generated** between areas of knowledge, especially through tasks such as elaboration.

78. Toker, D. (2015). *The most important sentence*. Retrieved from https://bit.ly/2PCfa2j

- Organising and simplifying images by using the three Cs of compare, contrast and categorise.
- Identifying and filling gaps in knowledge is the beginning of the process of **evaluation**.

In summary, the MARGE model can have a huge impact on students', teachers' and leaders' understanding of the learning process. It can help students better understand how they learn, help teachers refine their practice and help leaders ensure that the best conditions are in place to allow long-term learning to happen. Through gaining an insight into the neuroscience behind how the brain works and linking this with the latest research into cognitive science, MARGE allows teachers to affect the learning in their classrooms, pushing the point that learning is a whole-brain issue.

Concluding comments: Learning about learning through the MARGE model

When I first read Shimamura's book, *MARGE: A Whole-Brain Learning Approach for Students and Teachers*[79] I was taken aback by how much of it was already embedded in my teaching. Even after over a decade of teaching, I had previously struggled to explain why I did what I did in many of my lessons; MARGE gave me a framework to do this with more clarity.

One of the first lessons I taught after reading MARGE was on Newton's third law. By coincidence, I was being observed by a graduate who was interested in becoming a teacher.

I started the lesson with an introductory video; a 30-second clip of me in an indoor skydiving tunnel. In the video, I float in midair (with the assistance of an instructor) as a fan spins below me. At a key moment in the video, I realise that if I push down on the air with my arms, the air pushes back on me and I rise further up the wind tunnel. When playing this video to my students, they instantly engaged in a discussion with me about why I float and how I move. I explained that this is linked to the ideas of Newton's third law and led students to a set of summary questions, assessing their prior knowledge of forces. Once this was done, and I was confident their prior knowledge was at the level it needed to be, I provided a clear explanation of Newton's third law, ensuring that I was explicit about the parts of the explanation I wanted students to follow carefully. By providing them with a model explanation, which they could adjust and apply to a variety of scenarios, students could see how the knowledge

79. Shimamura, A. (2018)

they had just learned could be applied to the world around them. They could also relate what they had just learned to what they already knew about forces. Through a series of practice questions, students could self-test their application of the model answer not only within the lesson, but also within the homework I set.

When I asked the observer what they enjoyed about my lesson, they described that there were storytelling elements, that students knew how what they were doing fitted into the big picture of what they were learning, that a clear model was in place for students to use, and they were given a chance to practice using it and then evaluate its use. Through a simple conversation I was able to see how MARGE is not a bolt-on, but a framework around which to have constructive conversations around the learning process.

Shimamura states that it is his hope that we 'engage in lifelong learning well past your time as a student. Keep MARGE in mind whenever curiosity arises and the desire to learn comes upon you.'[80] He has reminded me that whatever age or stage in their career a learner is at, learning happens best when students are motivated, know what to attend to, can relate what they are learning to what they already know, have the opportunity to generate new links, and evaluate what they have learned. As Shimamura says: 'learning is a whole brain issue; it'll keep you active, should be fun, and it's best when it's shared with others'.[81]

80. Shimamura, A. (2018), p45
81. Shimamura, A. (2018), p46

BIBLIOGRAPHY

Agarwal, P. (2020). *Make flashcards more powerful with these 3 tips*. Retrieved from https://bit.ly/2PZ6WRw

Birbalsingh, K. (2016). *Battle Hymn of the Tiger Teachers*. Woodbridge: John Catt.

Bjork, R. (1994). Memory and meta-memory considerations in the training of human beings. In J. Metcalfe & A. Shimamura (Eds.) *Knowing about Knowing*. Cambridge, MA: MIT Press. Retrieved from https://bit.ly/3mlMOVQ

Brown, P., McDaniel, M., & Roediger, H. (2014). *Make it stick: the science of successful learning*. Cambridge, MA: Harvard University Press.

Caviglioli, O. (2019). *Dual Coding for Teachers*. Woodbridge: John Catt.

Chandler, P. & Sweller, J. (1992). The split attention effect as a factor in the design of instruction. *British Journal of Educational Psychology*, 62(2), 233-246.

Clark, R. & Lyons, C. (2004). *Graphics for learning: proven guidelines for planning, designing, and evaluating visuals in training materials*. Hoboken, NJ: Pfeiffer.

Colbran, S. (2018). *Flashcards and spaced repetition fending off forgetfulness*. Ascilite 2018. 10.13140/RG.2.2.16611.40485

Cornell University. (Retrieved 2020). *Cornell note-taking: note-taking strategies*. Cornell University. https://bit.ly/3wrorLc

Counsell, C. (2018, April 7). Senior Curriculum Leadership 1: The indirect manifestation of knowledge: (A) curriculum as narrative [Blog post]. Retrieved from https://bit.ly/3fBa9lg

Czekala, B. (2020). *Interleaved practice – when and how to use it to maximize learning pace*. Retrieved from https://bit.ly/3cPBq1y

Doebel, S. (2019). *How your brain's executive function works and how to improve it*. [Video file] Retrieved from https://youtu.be/qAC-5hTK-4c

Ebbinghaus, H. (2013). Memory: a contribution to experimental psychology. *Annals of neurosciences*, 20(4), 155-156. Retrieved from https://doi.org/10.5214/ans.0972.7531.200408

Epictetus. (2009). *The Golden Sayings of Epictetus* (H. Crossley, Trans.). EZreads Publications.

Forrin, N., MacLeod, C., & Ozubko, J. (2012). Widening the boundaries of the production effect. *Memory & cognition*, 40(7), 1046-1055. Retrieved from https://doi.org/10.3758/s13421-012-0210-8

Furst, E. (2018). Reconsolidation. *The life of a memory trace.* Retrieved from https://bit.ly/2QYvkDp

Furst, E. (2021). *Learning in the brain.* Retrieved from https://bit.ly/3rSY3Go

Hall, S. (2020, July 25). *Knowledge organisers – a failed revolution.* Retrieved from https://bit.ly/3mkQS8S

Hattie, J. (2013). *Visible learning and the science of how we learn.* Abingdon: Routledge.

Harvard, B. (2020). *Zooming in and out.* Retrieved from https://bit.ly/3cQLBCM

Jarry, J. (2020, December 27). T*he Dunning-Kruger effect is probably not real.* Retrieved from https://bit.ly/3dAwf4z

Jones, G. (2020, August 26). *Cornell versus Ebbinghaus.* Retrieved from https://bit.ly/3sSolKr

Khanna, M., Badura-Brack, A., & Finken, L. (2013). Short- and long-term effects of cumulative finals on student learning. *Teaching of Psychology*, 40(3), 175-182. Retrieved from https://doi.org/10.1177/0098628313487458

Kirby, J. (2015, May 3). *A 5-year revision plan.* Retrieved from https://bit.ly/3uq8Zgq

Klemm, W. (2017, December 15). *Enhance memory with the 'production effect'.* Retrieved from https://bit.ly/3sV7OW1

Lee, R. (2018, January 13). *On self-quizzing homework.* Retrieved from https://bit.ly/3cNTMQp

Lemov, D. (2015). *Teach Like a Champion 2.0.* San Francisco: Jossey-Bass.

Mccrea, P. (2018). *Learning what is it, and how might we catalyse it?* Retrieved from https://bit.ly/31LvgZT

Postman, L. (1976). Methodology in human learning. In W. K. Estes (Ed.) *Handbook of Learning and Cognitive Processes, Volume 3: Approaches to Human Learning and Motivation.* Hove: Psychology Press.

Rosenshine, B. (2012). Principles of instruction: research-based strategies that all teachers should know. *American Educator,* 36(1), 12-19. Retrieved from https://www.aft.org/sites/default/files/periodicals/Rosenshine.pdf

Rosner, Z., Elman, J., & Shimamura, A. (2013). The generation effect: activating broad neural circuits during memory encoding. *Cortex,* 49(7), 1901-1909. Retrieved from https://bit.ly/2PFFBEd

Sealy, C. (2020). *The researchED guide to the curriculum.* Woodbridge: John Catt.

Shimamura, A. (2018). *MARGE A whole-brain learning approach for students and teachers.* Retrieved from https://bit.ly/3rPxulE

Shimamura, A. (2018, July 21). *The power and pitfalls of brain-based learning programs.* Retrieved from https://bit.ly/3mmOE9g

Shimamura, A. (2020, June 5). *Do I Like It? Engage yourself with the 'aesthetic question.'* Retrieved from https://bit.ly/2PWLgpa

Shimamura, A. (2020, March 29). *Kids stuck at home?* Retrieved from https://bit.ly/3wtCj7C

Sundar, K. (2019). *Cut it out: learning with seductive details.* Retrieved from https://bit.ly/3wupPg8

Thomson, R. & Mehring, J. (2016). Better vocabulary study strategies for long-term learning. *Kwansei Gakuin University Humanities Review,* 20, 133-141.

Toker, D. (2015). *The most important sentence.* Retrieved from https://bit.ly/2PCfa2j

Weinstein, Y., Madam, C., & Sumcracki, M. (2018). Teaching the science of learning. *Cognitive Research: Principles and Implications,* (2). Retrieved from https://bit.ly/3mu5Z00

Willingham, D. T. (2010). *Why Don't Students Like School?* San Francisco: Jossey Bass.

Willingham, D. T. (2017, June 26). *On the definition of learning.* Retrieved from https://bit.ly/2PZGV4z

Wissman, K., Rawson, K., & Pyc, M. (2012). How and when do students use flashcards? *Memory,* 20(6), 568-579. Retrieved from https://doi.org/10.1080/09658211.2012.687052

Yonelinas, A., Wang, M., & Koen, J. (2010). Recollection and familiarity: examining controversial assumptions and new directions. *Hippocampus*, 20(11), 1178-1194. Retrieved from https://doi.org/10.1002/hipo.20864

Zormpa, E., Brehm, L., Hoedemaker, R., & Meyer, A. (2018). The production effect and the generation effect improve memory in picture naming. *Memory*, 27(3), 340-352. Retrieved from https://doi.org/10.1080/09658211.2018.1510966

CPSIA information can be obtained
at www.ICGtesting.com
Printed in the USA
JSHW051139210721
17054JS00001B/2

9 781913 622671